Presented to…

_____

On the Occasion of…

_____

From…

_____

BOSTON
uncommon

a culinary journey

through Boston's

distinctive

neighborhoods

A COOKBOOK

FROM THE

JUNIOR LEAGUE

OF BOSTON

BOSTON
*un*common

a culinary journey

through Boston's

distinctive

neighborhoods

BOSTON
uncommon

a culinary journey

through Boston's

distinctive

neighborhoods

Published by
The Junior League of Boston

Copyright © 2007
The Junior League of Boston
117 Newbury Street
Boston, Massachusetts 02116
www.JLBoston.org

Photography: © Nina Gallant

This cookbook is a collection of favorite recipes, which are not necessarily original recipes.

Library of Congress number:
2006922256
ISBN: 0-9778059-0-5

Edited, Designed, and Manufactured by
Favorite Recipes® Press
An imprint of

FRP™

P.O. Box 305142
Nashville, Tennessee 37230
1-800-358-0560

Art Director: Steve Newman
Book Designer: David Malone
Project Editor: Susan Larson

Manufactured in China
First Printing 2007 10,000 copies

table of contents

acknowledgments

It is with tremendous gratitude that the Junior League of Boston would like to thank
our primary sponsor, DUNKIN' BRANDS, for their generosity and support.
Since 1950 Dunkin' Donuts has been a part of Boston and its neighborhoods.
Today, it is the largest coffee and baked goods chain in the world.
Please visit them in a neighborhood near you or at www.dunkindonuts.com.

With special thanks to all of our sponsors
Dunkin' Brands
The Boston Beer Company
On Holiday, LLC
Mr. and Mrs. William Berutti

Photography
Nina Gallant

Photographer Nina Gallant is an area native and happily lives, eats,
and photographs in Boston. She attributes her appreciation of
good food to her family and her love of photography to life.
Her work can also be viewed at www.ninagallant.com.

Food Styling
Dave Becker   Diane Baxter

Cover Design and Illustrations
Kerren Barbas

acknowledgments

Cookbook Advisory Committee

Pamela Berutti

Erin Clement

Karen DiMarzo

Jessica Grosman

Mary Kittell

Nissa Knight

Karen Roth LoRusso

Lisa Macchi

Katherine Menzia

Tatum Pyle

Cookbook Committee 2002–2006

Tara Auclair

Kerren Barbas

Sarah Ruth Barnard

Pamela Berutti

Cara Mia Bruncati

Elizabeth Butcher

Lisa Candy

Erin Clement

Sarah Cunningham

Alice Davidson

Karen DiMarzo

Linnea Dreslin

Catharine Ebling

Brooke Gallo

Kristin Greene

Jessica Grosman

Jennifer Guebert

Leanne Hannon

Haidee Heyward

Hollie Hurwitch

Heather Jackson

Cindy Joyce

Nina Jung

Mary Kittell

Nissa Knight

Paula LaMarche

Meredith Levin

Karen Roth LoRusso

Kerry Lynch

Lisa Macchi

Catherine Madden

Kimberly McKillop

Katherine Menzia

Stephanie Murphy

April Paterno

Kimberly Pope

Stephanie Price

Tatum Pyle

Margaret Rutter

Britt Sanford

Lynne Schaffer

Heather Shaff Beaver

Karen Skinner

Amelia Slawsby

Joanna Stimson

Allison Thies

Jane Timothy

Kelly Wesley

Danielle West

Heather Whelehan

Nora Wilkes

Special Recognition

Valerie Albrecht

Anne Benning

Cherie Bosarge Dutton

Amy Cohen

Sarah Cunningham

Hilary Forbes

Hannah Gilligan

Kirby Lunger

Elizabeth Tyminski

introduction

To coincide with the United States' bicentennial in 1976, the Junior League of Boston published its first cookbook, *The Boston Tea Party*. Now, the JLB will celebrate its own centennial with the publication of its newest cookbook, *Boston Uncommon*.

As a lifelong resident of the greater Boston area, I am so proud to introduce a cookbook that highlights the best of Boston through food, facts, and photos. *Boston Uncommon* is a virtual cornucopia of the incredibly varied cuisine that Boston offers, emphasizing local ingredients and celebrated chefs. Information about Boston and its many neighborhoods has been sprinkled throughout to give you a flavor of this beautiful city.

To bring you this tasteful collection, the members of the JLB's Cookbook Committee have solicited and tested hundreds of recipes from the JLB membership during the last four years. Their enthusiasm has even inspired many of those less culinarily inclined to spend more time in the kitchen. In fact, this year I personally hosted our family holiday dinner for the first time!

The incredible effort put into this cookbook is a testament to the commitment of our members . . . They knew that the proceeds of this cookbook would directly help us support our mission: *The Junior League of Boston is an organization of women committed to promoting voluntarism, developing the potential of women, and improving communities through the effective action and leadership of trained volunteers. Its purpose is exclusively educational and charitable.*

For the last one hundred years, our members have been a part of the rich history of the greater Boston community—so, while reading in the coming pages about the Bunker Hill monument in Charlestown, the seven-mile Emerald Necklace that stretches out to Brookline, or the "Chocolate Village" in Dorchester, know that our volunteers strive to continually improve lives in each of these communities.

When Sarah Lawrence founded the Junior League of Boston in 1907, she and a group of young women were inspired to address the social and industrial problems of Boston at the turn of the century. In addition to establishing a lecture series on topics of grave importance to Boston, volunteers were sent throughout the city to visit and assist the sick and the elderly. Later, members helped in hospitals, produced a film nationally recognized for its contributions to public understanding of the mentally challenged, published the *Guide to Boston for the Handicapped*, and established—and ran—a child abuse center.

Now, a century later, nearly 1,300 member volunteers participate in training and voluntarism to promote change for the better in each of four specific initiatives: college and career counseling, combating domestic violence, health advocacy, and the positive development of adolescent girls.

The women of the JLB give generously of their time, their talents, and their treasures to support eighteen community service projects that tremendously impact the health and education of women and children in the greater Boston area.

Within *Boston Uncommon* you will find a variety of recipes reflecting the culture of New England as well as the style of Boston. I know that this delicious endeavor will provide you with many hours of entertainment, whether trying a new recipe, enjoying a perfect version of an old favorite, or simply feasting on the insight provided about this fabulous city. Savor the knowledge that your support of this cookbook makes our work possible.

—Elizabeth Tyminski, JLB President 2005–2006

think beyond the cork
COMPLEMENTING YOUR MEAL WITH THE RIGHT BEER

I would invite you to think beyond the cork. The world of beer is a rich and diverse place. Though wine may be your first thought for pairing with food, beer can be the perfect choice to enjoy with a meal.

Beer has several advantages. First, its lower alcohol content means it will not overwhelm the flavor of the food, but will blend with and complement your meal. Second, most beer is not as acidic or tannic as wine. Excessive acidity and astringency may overwhelm the delicate flavors the chef wants to accentuate. Third, beer has a huge flavor spectrum because of its variety of ingredients. Beer may include different grains and roasts of those grains; different varietals of hops, spices, and fruits; and a variety of different yeasts. This array of ingredients leads to a wide variety of flavors. There is a beer to match and complement any cuisine! Finally, beer is fun. Try this at home: Next time you have a dinner party and need a cool new twist, get a mix of beers from different states or countries and explore the world of beer. From cheeses to pâté, dinner to your favorite chocolate dessert, there's a beer that will complement every dish!

For more information about food and beer pairings or about visiting our Boston brewery, see our information in the Resource Guide. Cheers!

—Jim Koch, Founder and Brewer of Samuel Adams® Beer

Goat Cheese Torta with Pesto and Sun-dried Tomatoes

APPETIZERS
& cocktails

Both historic and cosmopolitan, the South End and Back Bay have it all. The South End was once a strip of land surrounded by a magnificent bay and tidal flats. The topography of the area caused it to be known as "Boston's neck." The South End has changed considerably since 1770, when only a few mansions dotted its landscape. In 1833, the area was expanded by seventy acres of landfill. Today, this once sparsely populated neighborhood has nearly 35,000 residences and approximately one square mile of parks, fountains, and beautiful architecture. The South End is a historically registered neighborhood that has the largest collection of original Victorian-style, bowfront, row houses in the United States.

Located in the heart of the city, this picturesque neighborhood is known for its active residents. The South End boasts more than twenty neighborhood associations and regularly sponsors community-based activities. But the South End is also known for its food. Wine shops, specialty cheese shops, cafes, bakeries, and trendy restaurant-bars are nestled among renovated brick-front buildings along tree-lined streets. Appetizers and drinks with friends can be one of the best ways to

sample the variety of dining options offered in this neighborhood. Be sure to explore the South End; go off the beaten path and experience cosmopolitan dining with a neighborhood feel.

The historic Back Bay neighbors the South End. Like the South End, the 580-acre Back Bay is 100 percent landfill. In 1820, two mountains sacrificed from the Beacon Hill area were used to create the Back Bay. It took fifty years to complete the project of filling in the Back Bay. Because they were built on landfill, buildings in the Back Bay are uniquely constructed, connected by pilings to base rock to prevent sinking.

The Back Bay reflects a unique combination of the old and the new. Historic Trinity Church in Copley Square sits adjacent to the sleek John Hancock Tower. The Boston Marathon, first held in 1897, is considered by many to be the most prestigious marathon in the country. It takes place annually and finishes in the heart of the Back Bay. Nearby is Newbury Street, lined with high-fashion specialty shops, outdoor cafes, and bistros—providing the perfect location to see and be seen while sipping a cappuccino or dining alfresco.

The Back Bay is home to the headquarters of the Junior League of Boston. Like the Back Bay itself, the Junior League of Boston is an incredible blend of history and change. Founded in 1906 as a women's sewing circle, the Junior League of Boston is the second oldest Junior League in America. Today, more than 1,200 Junior League of Boston volunteers offer their time and talent to strengthen the community and enrich the lives of others.

The South End and Back Bay are truly unique. Whether your dining or shopping preference is upscale or casual, the South End and Back Bay offer something for everybody.

goat cheese torta
with pesto and sun-dried tomatoes

12   ounces goat cheese or chèvre, softened, cut into pieces
1   cup (2 sticks) unsalted butter, softened, cut into pieces
8   ounces cream cheese, softened, cut into pieces
2   tablespoons dry vermouth
1   shallot, minced
2   garlic cloves, minced
>   Hot red pepper sauce to taste (optional)
1   cup (8 ounces) homemade or purchased pesto
1   cup (8 ounces) oil-pack sun-dried tomatoes, drained, minced
>   Fresh basil leaves for garnish
>   Baguette slices or crackers

Leftover torta may be tossed with warm linguini and garnished with fresh basil leaves for a delicious and colorful pasta dish.

Combine the goat cheese, butter, cream cheese, vermouth, shallot and garlic in a food processor and process until smooth. Season with pepper sauce.

Oil a 4- to 5-cup straight-sided mold or loaf pan; line with plastic wrap, letting 1 inch of the wrap extend over each side. Spread 1/3 of the cheese mixture in the prepared pan. Top evenly with the pesto, 1/2 of the remaining cheese mixture and the sun-dried tomatoes; pack down gently. Spread with the remaining cheese mixture. Fold the plastic wrap over the top; press gently to compact the layers. Refrigerate for at least 2 hours. (May be prepared in advance and refrigerated for up to 5 days or frozen for up to 3 months. If frozen, thaw overnight in the refrigerator.)

Uncover and invert onto a serving dish. Carefully remove the plastic wrap. Garnish with basil leaves. Serve with baguette slices or crackers.

Serves 20   *Photo on page 10*

Uncommonly Boston — First run in 1897, the Boston Marathon is America's oldest and one of the most prestigious marathons.

spanakopita
(greek spinach pie)

4	tablespoons olive oil	1	bunch dill weed, chopped
1 1/2	tablespoons butter	12	ounces feta cheese, cut into small pieces
2	Spanish onions, chopped		
2	leeks, white and light green parts only, chopped	8	ounces ricotta cheese
1	small anise bulb, chopped	12	extra-large eggs
>	Pepper to taste	14	to 16 sheets frozen phyllo dough, thawed
1	pound fresh spinach, chopped	1/2	cup (about) melted butter

Heat the olive oil and 1 1/2 tablespoons butter in a large pot over medium heat. Add the onions, leeks and anise. Cook for 7 to 10 minutes or just until tender. Season with pepper. Add the spinach and dill weed. Cook for 5 to 10 minutes or until the spinach is wilted. Cool; drain any excess liquid.

Combine the feta cheese and ricotta cheese in a bowl. Beat the eggs in a mixing bowl. Add the cheese mixture and beat well. Add the spinach mixture and stir in by hand.

Butter an 11×17-inch baking pan. Layer seven to eight sheets of phyllo dough in the prepared pan, brushing each sheet with melted butter, making sure the phyllo dough extends over the sides of the pan to cover the rim and forms a small crust around the edges. Spread the spinach mixture evenly over the phyllo in the pan. Layer the remaining seven to eight sheets of phyllo dough on top, brushing each sheet, including the top, with butter. Score the top into serving-size portions, but do not cut all the way down into the spinach filling.

Bake at 350 degrees for about 1 hour or until golden brown.

Serves 30

 Uncommonly Boston — Boston's famous Swan Boats, invented in 1877, paddle under the "world's smallest suspension bridge," the Public Garden Bridge.

stuffed brie

For something unexpected, pair this delicious stuffed Brie cheese with Dunkin' Donuts Toasted Almond Vanilla Coffee and wow your guests!

1	(6-inch) wheel Brie cheese or Camembert cheese	3	tablespoons chopped walnuts
1	small Granny Smith apple, thinly sliced	3	tablespoons whiskey or bourbon
3	tablespoons brown sugar	>	Stone-ground wheat crackers, baguette slices or apple and pear slices

Slice the cheese lengthwise into halves. Layer 1/2 of the apple slices on the cut side of the bottom cheese half. Combine the brown sugar, walnuts and whiskey in a small mixing bowl. Spread evenly over the layered apples. Top with the remaining apple slices. Cover with the top cheese half, rind side up. Place on a baking sheet.

Bake at 400 degrees for 5 to 10 minutes or until the cheese melts to the desired consistency. Serve with crackers, baguette slices or apple and pear slices.

Serves 4 to 6

artichoke crostini with brie

This is a perfect appetizer for a cocktail party or buffet table.

1	(12-ounce) can artichokes	>	Olive oil (optional)
5	large basil leaves	4	ounces Brie cheese, cut into 25 thin slices
1	or 2 garlic cloves		
1	loaf French bread, cut into 25 slices		

Drain the artichokes, reserving the liquid. Process the artichokes, basil and garlic in a food processor or blender; set aside.

Arrange the bread slices on a baking sheet. Brush with the reserved artichoke liquid or olive oil. Spread the artichoke mixture evenly over the bread. Top each with a cheese slice.

Bake at 400 degrees for 10 to 12 minutes or until the cheese is melted and browned.

Serves 25

grilled vegetable roulades

These grilled vegetable bundles, served with a tangy dipping sauce, are warm and savory.

When choosing appetizers to serve at a cocktail party, make selections that are simple, flavorful, and easily handled. Guests will appreciate delicious tidbits that keep their hands free and don't require cutlery and china.

2 1/2	cups balsamic vinegar
1	teaspoon honey
1	teaspoon grated orange zest
10	(1/4-inch-thick) lengthwise slices zucchini
10	(1/4-inch-thick) lengthwise slices summer squash
10	(1/4-inch-thick) lengthwise slices eggplant
>	Olive oil
>	Salt and pepper to taste
8	to 10 thin slices prosciutto
1	(8-ounce) jar roasted red peppers, drained, cut into strips
1	(6-ounce) container buffalo mozzarella cheese, sliced 1/8 inch thick (about 2 to 3 balls)

Combine the vinegar, honey and orange zest in a medium saucepan. Bring to a boil over medium heat. Reduce the heat to low. Simmer for about 20 minutes or until the liquid is reduced by 1/2 to 3/4 and is the consistency of syrup. Pour into a bowl. Let stand until cool. Place the zucchini, summer squash and eggplant on a baking sheet. Drizzle lightly with olive oil; toss until all the surfaces are lightly coated. Sprinkle with salt and pepper. Heat a grill or grill pan until hot. Grill the vegetables for 1 to 2 minutes on each side or until tender. Place on a baking sheet. Let stand until cool.

Cut the prosciutto slices into strips about the same width as the vegetables. For each roulade, layer a prosciutto slice and red pepper strip on a grilled vegetable; place a cheese slice near one end. Starting at the short end and ending at the cheese end, roll up to create a bundle. Secure with a wooden pick. Repeat with the remaining ingredients.

Grill the roulades just until the cheese starts to melt. (You may place them on a microwave-safe dish and microwave on Low for 10 to 20 seconds.) Place the warm roulades on a serving plate. Drizzle with the balsamic syrup.

Serves 8 to 10

caramelized onion
and gorgonzola appetizer

This appetizer makes a flavorful accompaniment to soup and salad.

1/4 cup (1/2 stick) butter	1 (16-ounce) Italian bread shell
4 large sweet onions, sliced	1 cup Gorgonzola cheese, crumbled
> Pinch of sugar	1 cup macadamia nuts, chopped
> Salt and pepper to taste	

Melt the butter in a large skillet over medium-low heat. Add the onions. Sauté for 15 to 20 minutes or until caramelized. Stir in the sugar, salt and pepper. Spread the onions over the bread shell. Top with the cheese and macadamia nuts.

Bake at 450 degrees for 10 minutes. Cut into small strips or bite-size squares.

Serves 8 to 12

healthy apricot appetizer

2 cups orange juice	4 ounces chèvre or goat cheese
36 dried apricots	1/2 cup pistachios, coarsely chopped

Heat the orange juice in a microwave oven or on top of the stove until warm, but not hot. Add the apricots; let soak for 30 minutes. Drain the apricots, discarding the juice.

Spread the cheese evenly over the apricots. Dip the apricots, cheese side down, into the pistachios, pressing firmly to coat well. Arrange the apricots on a serving dish. Refrigerate, covered, until ready to serve.

Serves 6 to 8

Uncommonly Boston — Founded in 1848, the Boston Public Library was the first free American public library.

tapenade on crostini

1	cup pitted Spanish green olives	1/2	teaspoon herbes de Provence
1 3/4	cups pitted black olives	1	baguette, cut into 1/4-inch-thick slices
2	tablespoons extra-virgin olive oil	1/4	cup balsamic vinegar
3	garlic cloves, minced, or to taste	1/4	cup extra-virgin olive oil
3	fresh sage leaves, minced	>	Salt and pepper to taste

Combine the green olives, black olives, 2 tablespoons olive oil, garlic, sage and herbes de Provence in a food processor and pulse until slightly chunky or to desired consistency; set aside. Place the baguette slices on a baking sheet. Combine the vinegar, 1/4 cup olive oil, salt and pepper in a bowl. Brush generously over both sides of the bread. Broil the bread for 1 minute on each side or until lightly browned. Serve with the tapenade.

Serves 4 to 6

three-pepper quesadillas

Try pairing this appetizer favorite with rich Samuel Adams Boston Ale any time of the year or with Samuel Adams Summer Ale during the warmer months.

1	tablespoon olive oil	1/2	teaspoon cumin
1	cup thinly sliced red bell pepper strips	8	ounces cream cheese, softened
1	cup thinly sliced green bell pepper strips	2	cups (8 ounces) shredded Cheddar cheese
1	cup thinly sliced yellow bell pepper strips	1/2	cup (2 ounces) grated Parmesan cheese
1/2	cup thinly sliced onion	10	(6-inch) flour tortillas

Heat the olive oil in a large skillet. Add the bell peppers and onion. Sauté to desired doneness. Stir in the cumin; set aside.

Beat the cream cheese, Cheddar cheese and Parmesan cheese in a mixing bowl until well mixed. For each quesadilla, spread 2 tablespoons of the cheese mixture on a tortilla. Top with a spoonful of the pepper mixture. Fold the tortilla in half. Place the quesadillas on a baking sheet. Bake at 425 degrees for 10 minutes. Cut each quesadilla into thirds.

Serves 30

stuffed mushrooms

24	large mushrooms	3	garlic cloves, minced
1/4	cup (1/2 stick) butter	1/2	cup fine dry bread crumbs
4	ounces sweet Italian sausage	1/2	cup crumbled blue cheese
1/2	cup diced onion		

Clean the mushrooms. Remove the stems and chop enough to measure 1 cup. Set aside the mushroom caps.

Melt the butter in a medium saucepan. Add the chopped mushroom stems, sausage, onion and garlic. Sauté until the vegetables are tender and the sausage is cooked through. Remove from the heat. Stir in the bread crumbs and cheese. Spoon evenly into the mushroom caps. Place on a baking sheet. Bake at 425 degrees for 10 minutes or until heated through.

Serves 24

prosciutto and swiss hors d'oeuvre

3/4	cup (3 ounces) finely shredded Swiss cheese	1/2	(17-ounce) package frozen puff pastry (1 sheet), thawed, cut lengthwise into halves
4	teaspoons chopped fresh sage leaves, or 2 teaspoons dried sage	2	ounces thinly sliced prosciutto
1	egg, beaten	>	Mango chutney or fruit preserves

Combine the cheese and sage in a bowl. Brush some of the egg along one long edge of each pastry half. Arrange 1/2 of the prosciutto slices evenly over the pastry, leaving the egg-brushed edge uncovered. Sprinkle 1/2 of the cheese mixture over the prosciutto. Roll up the pastry, beginning at the unbrushed long edge, into a log. Press the egg-brushed edge to seal. Wrap the log in plastic wrap. Repeat with the remaining ingredients. Chill the logs, seam side down, at least 3 hours or for up to 3 days.

Lightly grease two baking sheets. Cut the logs into 1/2-inch-thick slices. Arrange the slices, cut side down, 1 inch apart on the baking sheets. Bake at 400 degrees for 14 to 16 minutes or until golden brown. Cool slightly on a wire rack. Spoon a dab of chutney or preserves on each slice. Serve warm.

Serves 40

deviled eggs with smoked salmon
and capers

9	hard-cooked eggs	1	tablespoon capers, chopped
2	ounces smoked salmon, chopped	2	teaspoons fresh lemon juice
5	tablespoons mayonnaise	>	Salt to taste

Slice the eggs lengthwise into halves; remove the yolks and place in a bowl. Mash the yolks with a fork until smooth. Add the salmon, mayonnaise, capers and lemon juice and mix well. Season with salt. Spoon the yolk mixture into the egg whites. Arrange on a serving platter.

Serves 18   *Photo on page 21*

shrimp won tons

4	ounces fresh deveined peeled shrimp, finely chopped	$1/2$	teaspoon salt
		$1/4$	teaspoon sesame oil
2	ounces lean ground pork	>	Dash of white pepper
3	whole water chestnuts, finely chopped	24	won ton wrappers
2	green onions, chopped	>	Vegetable oil for deep-frying
1	teaspoon cornstarch	>	Sweet-and-sour sauce

Combine the first 8 ingredients in a large bowl. Place $1/2$ teaspoon of the shrimp mixture in the center of a won ton wrapper. Fold the bottom corner of the wrapper over the filling, forming a triangle. Brush the right corner of the triangle with water to moisten. Bring the bottom corners together below the filling, overlapping them slightly and pinching the left corner to the right corner to seal. Heat $1 1/2$ inches vegetable oil in a wok to 350 degrees. Add four or five won tons at a time. Fry for 3 minutes or until golden brown, turning two or three times. Drain on paper towels. Serve with sweet-and-sour sauce.

Serves 24

miniature spicy crab cakes

CHEF MING TSAI   Blue Ginger

Owners Ming and Polly Tsai have created a stunning dining space that incorporates soothing natural elements and the principles of feng shui. The open kitchen sets the perfect stage for creating their signature East-West dishes. The unique cuisine and memorable dining experience continue to impress diners and earn them some of the culinary world's highest honors.

1/2	cup best-quality mayonnaise
2	tablespoons sambal oelek (a Southeast Asian hot chile pepper paste)
2	tablespoons chopped fresh chives
1	pound lump crab meat, shells and cartilage removed
>	Juice of 1 lime

1	teaspoon honey
>	Kosher salt and freshly ground pepper to taste
1	cup flour
3	extra-large eggs, lightly beaten
1	cup panko or plain dry bread crumbs
>	Grapeseed oil or canola oil

Combine 1/4 cup of the mayonnaise, 1 tablespoon of the sambal oelek and 1 tablespoon of the chives in a small bowl and mix well.

Combine the remaining 1/4 cup mayonnaise, 1 tablespoon sambal oelek, the crab meat, lime juice and honey in a medium bowl. Season with salt and pepper. For each crab cake, shape 2 tablespoons of the crab mixture with moistened hands into a cake, packing tightly. Place the flour, eggs and bread crumbs in three separate deep plates. Dredge the crab cakes in the flour, then dip in the eggs and dredge in the bread crumbs to coat.

Heat a large sauté pan over high heat. Add the grapeseed oil to the pan, swirling to coat the bottom. Add the crab cakes. Cook for about 2 minutes on each side or until browned and crisp and cooked through. Drain on a paper towel-lined plate. Drizzle the reserved mayonnaise mixture on a serving platter in a zigzag pattern; top with the crab cakes. Garnish with the remaining 1 tablespoon chives.

Serves 16

Uncommonly Boston — The first paid municipal fire department in North America was created in Boston in 1678.

artichoke dip

12	ounces cream cheese, softened		2	cups drained artichoke hearts, patted dry
1/2	cup milk or half-and-half		1	teaspoon kosher salt
1/2	cup (2 ounces) freshly grated Parmesan cheese		>	Pinch of cayenne pepper
2	scallions, white and green parts, chopped		>	Freshly ground black pepper to taste
1	egg, beaten		>	Pinch of paprika
1	tablespoon fresh lemon juice		>	Assorted crackers or toasted baguette slices
1	garlic clove, minced			

Combine the cream cheese, milk, Parmesan cheese, scallions, egg, lemon juice and garlic in a food processor and pulse until smooth. Add the artichokes, salt, cayenne pepper and black pepper and pulse until mixed but still chunky. Spoon into a buttered 1-quart baking dish. Sprinkle with the paprika.

Bake at 350 degrees for about 1 hour or until lightly browned and set. Serve warm with crackers or baguette slices.

Serves 12

green monster dip

1	(10-ounce) package frozen chopped spinach, thawed, drained		1	(8-ounce) can sliced water chestnuts, chopped
1 1/4	cups (5 ounces) freshly grated Parmesan cheese		1	roasted red pepper, chopped
1 1/4	cups mayonnaise		1	garlic clove, minced
1	(14-ounce) jar marinated artichoke hearts, drained, chopped		>	Stone-ground wheat crackers

Combine the spinach, cheese, mayonnaise, artichoke hearts, water chestnuts, red pepper and garlic in a bowl and mix well. Spoon into a pie plate or shallow baking dish. Bake at 350 degrees for 20 minutes or until lightly browned. Serve warm with crackers.

Serves 12 to 16

creamy hearts of palm dip

Hearts of palm are a great substitute for artichokes. Keep a jar on hand for dips, salads, and stir-fries.

1	(15-ounce) can hearts of palm, drained, finely chopped	1/2	cup finely chopped roasted red pepper
1	cup (4 ounces) grated Parmesan cheese	1	garlic clove, finely chopped
3/4	cup mayonnaise	1/4	cup slivered almonds
1/2	cup fresh bread crumbs	>	Crackers, pita bread or French bread

Combine the hearts of palm, cheese, mayonnaise, bread crumbs, red pepper and garlic in a bowl. Spoon into a small baking dish. Bake at 350 degrees for 15 minutes or until heated through. Top with the almonds. Bake for 10 minutes longer. Serve hot with crackers, pita bread or French bread.

Serves 10

roquefort mousse

A full-bodied cabernet beautifully complements this melt-in-your-mouth mousse.

4	to 6 ounces Roquefort cheese, softened	1/2	cup heavy whipping cream
4	ounces cream cheese, softened	1/4	cup pecans, chopped
1/4	cup (1/2 stick) butter, softened	1/4	cup fresh parsley, chopped
1 1/2	tablespoons Cognac	2	apples, sliced (such as Granny Smith)
1	garlic clove, minced	2	pears, sliced (such as red pears)

Line a small bowl or mold with plastic wrap, letting 1 inch of the wrap extend over the side. Combine the Roquefort cheese, cream cheese, butter, Cognac and garlic in a bowl and mix well with a fork. Beat the cream in a mixing bowl until stiff peaks form. Fold into the cheese mixture. Press into the prepared bowl. Fold the plastic wrap over the top. Refrigerate for 30 minutes.

Unmold the mousse onto a plate and carefully remove the plastic wrap. Garnish with the pecans and parsley. Arrange the apples and pears around the mousse before serving.

Serves 10 to 12

vidalia onion dip

1 cup diced Vidalia onion

1 cup (4 ounces) shredded Cheddar cheese

1 cup mayonnaise or light mayonnaise

> Crackers or crostini

Combine the onion, cheese and mayonnaise in a mixing bowl. Spoon into a greased baking dish. Bake at 350 degrees for 30 to 45 minutes or until browned and bubbly. Serve with crackers or crostini.

Serves 6 to 8

mint pesto

This tasty recipe is a great way to use the extra mint from your herb garden.

1/2 cup golden raisins

2 small shallots

2 cups firmly packed fresh mint leaves

2 tablespoons chopped walnuts

6 tablespoons whipped cream cheese

2 tablespoons olive oil

> Pita bread wedges

Combine the raisins and shallots in a food processor and process until coarsely chopped. Add the mint and walnuts and pulse until the mint is coarsely chopped. Add the cream cheese and olive oil and pulse until well mixed. Serve with plain or lightly toasted pita bread wedges.

Serves 6 to 8

 Uncommonly Boston — The first commercial bakery was opened just north of Boston by John Pearson in 1792.

liver pâté

Serve pâté as a delicious bagel spread for brunch. Or, top a simple salad of mixed greens with a small wedge of pâté for a rich luncheon alternative.

1/4	cup (1/2 stick) butter	1/2	teaspoon pepper
1	onion, diced (about 1 cup)	2	tablespoons (heaping) sour cream or buttermilk salad dressing
1	pound chicken livers		
1/2	cup red wine	>	Cherry tomato halves or red bell pepper slices for garnish
1	tablespoon Worcestershire sauce		
1/2	teaspoon salt	>	Crackers, cocktail rye bread slices or crostini
1/2	teaspoon garlic powder		

Melt the butter in a large sauté pan. Add the onion. Sauté until tender. Add the chicken livers, wine, Worcestershire sauce, salt, garlic powder and pepper. Sauté for 15 minutes or until the chicken livers are no longer pink in the center and most of the liquid has evaporated. Remove from the heat. Mash the liver mixture with a fork. Stir in the sour cream. Spoon into a serving bowl. Refrigerate, covered, for 8 to 12 hours. Garnish with cherry tomato halves or bell pepper slices. Serve with crackers, cocktail rye bread or crostini.

Serves 6 to 8

spiced pecans

1	egg white	1/2	teaspoon salt
1	teaspoon water	1/2	teaspoon cinnamon
1	pound pecan halves	>	Dash of nutmeg
1	cup sugar		

Whisk the egg white and water in a medium bowl until frothy. Add the pecans and stir to coat. Combine the sugar, salt, cinnamon and nutmeg in a separate bowl. Pour over the pecans and stir to coat. Spread the pecans on a foil-lined baking sheet. Bake at 250 degrees for 1 hour, stirring every 15 minutes. Serve at room temperature or freeze until ready to use.

Serves 10

red-nosed reindeer

1   ounce cranberry vodka

6   ounces ginger ale

3   ice cubes

>   Lime wedge for garnish

Combine the vodka and ginger ale in a cocktail shaker with ice cubes. Shake well and pour into a chilled glass. Garnish with a lime wedge.

Serves 1

summer splendor

1   part Pimm's

>   Ice cubes

3   parts freshly made lemonade

>   Fresh mint sprigs

>   Orange slice for garnish

Pour the Pimm's into a tall glass. Fill the glass with ice cubes. Pour the lemonade over the ice almost to the top of the glass. Add mint sprigs to taste and stir. Garnish with an orange slice.

Serves 1

Uncommonly Boston — Cranberry juice is the official beverage of the Commonwealth of Massachusetts.

candy cane martini

When making a shaken drink, such as a martini, a glass jar with a tight-fitting lid may be substituted for a cocktail shaker. Place the ice in the jar, add the liquid ingredients, put on the lid, and shake. Remove the lid and pour the chilled cocktail through a strainer into a classic martini glass.

> Cranberry juice
> Small candy canes, finely crushed

1 1/2 ounces premium vodka

1 teaspoon peppermint schnapps, or more to taste

> Ice

Moisten the rim of a chilled cocktail glass with cranberry juice; dip in crushed candy canes to coat.

Combine the vodka, schnapps and a splash of cranberry juice in a cocktail shaker with ice. Strain into the prepared cocktail glass. Serve immediately.

Serves 1   *Photo on page 29*

rasmopolitan

3 ice cubes

1 1/2 ounces cranberry-raspberry juice

1 ounce raspberry-flavored vodka

1/2 ounce Cointreau

> Juice of 1/2 lime
> Lime wedge for garnish

Combine the ice cubes, cranberry-raspberry juice, vodka, Cointreau and lime juice in a cocktail shaker. Shake well and strain into a martini glass. Garnish the edge of the glass with a lime wedge. Serve immediately.

Serves 1

castle island cooler

- > Cranberry juice
- > Orange juice
- > Pineapple juice
- > Club soda
- > Mount Gay Rum
- > Captain Morgan's Spiced Rum
- > Myer's Dark Rum
- > Key limes
- > Ice

Combine 4 parts cranberry juice, 1 part orange juice, 2 parts pineapple juice, 1 part club soda, 2 parts Mount Gay Rum, 1 part Captain Morgan's Rum, $1/2$ part Myer's Dark Rum, 1 lime per part and ice in a pitcher and stir to combine.

Variable servings

fall rum punch

60	cloves	2/3	cup sugar
6	oranges	>	Cinnamon
1	quart dark rum	>	Nutmeg
2	quarts apple cider		

Push 10 cloves into each orange. Place the oranges on a baking sheet. Bake at 325 degrees until juices begin to run. Place the oranges in a large pot with a lid. Add the rum. Cook over low heat until the rum is warm. Add the cider and sugar. Bring to a boil. Remove from the heat and ignite the punch. Sprinkle with cinnamon and nutmeg after the flames have subsided.

Serves 12

Uncommonly Boston — The first regularly issued newspaper was published in Boston in 1704.

perfect pink party punch

1   to 2 (12-ounce) packages frozen raspberries
3   (12-ounce) cans frozen pink lemonade concentrate
3   (2-liter) bottles ginger ale

One to two days before serving, fill a bundt pan ⅓ full with water. Add 1 package raspberries and freeze. Just before serving, run hot water over the pan. Remove the ice ring and place it carefully in a punch bowl. (For long events, make a second ice ring.) Add 2 cans of the lemonade concentrate and 2 bottles of the ginger ale to the punch bowl. (The punch will fizz up.) Replenish the punch bowl with the remaining lemonade concentrate, ginger ale and ice ring if necessary.

Serves 30

sunny champagne punch

1   lemon
¼   cup sugar
2   (12-ounce) cans frozen lemonade concentrate
2   (12-ounce) cans frozen white grape juice concentrate

>   Juice of 1 lemon
2   (750-milliliter) bottles Champagne or sparkling wine, chilled
>   Ice

Cut the lemon into ¼-inch-thick slices. Cut each slice into halves to form wedges. Place the sugar on a plate. Dip both sides of the lemon wedges into the sugar to coat; set aside. Combine the lemonade and grape juice concentrates in a punch bowl. Add the lemon juice, Champagne and ice. Serve in punch cups garnished with the sugared lemon wedges.

Notes: Recipe may be cut in half. The concentrates and lemon juice may be combined in advance. Add the Champagne and ice just before serving.

Serves 15 to 20

Hearty Fish Chowder

SOUPS & chowders

Rich in culture, Chinatown is one of Boston's unique neighborhoods. Located between South Station and the Theatre District, Boston's Chinatown is the third largest in the nation. The 1882 Exclusion Act prohibited Chinese laborers from entering the United States, so middle-class Irish and other people of European descent originally settled the area now known as Chinatown. It wasn't until the early 1900s that Chinese moved into the area. Railroads and leather factories brought jobs to Boston, which offered opportunity to new Chinese immigrants. Where other immigrant populations typically brought entire families to the United States, resourceful Chinese males relocated to America to work and send money back to support their families. By the early 1960s, many ethnic Chinese moved out of the neighborhood, and Southeast Asians moved in. Today, many Asian cultures, including Vietnamese, Cantonese, Cambodian, Thai, and Korean, inhabit the small number of city blocks designated as Chinatown.

The community gardens, located off Berkley Street, are a living example of Chinatown's multicultural influences. The culinary preferences and agricultural traditions of each immigrant population are reflected in the variety of fresh vegetables, fruits, and flowers cultivated. Boston's Chinatown undoubtedly has some of the best Asian cuisine in the city. The Hong Far Low restaurant, established in 1879, was one of the first restaurants in Chinatown. The streets of Chinatown offer gastronomic delights: Chinese bakeries display delicate pastries; butcher shops offer live poultry, fish, and succulent roasted duck; fruit and vegetable merchants display fresh Asian produce; herbalists offer cooking spices and natural remedies. Dim sum is another culinary experience that allows you to sample a variety of fare. Most restaurants offer dim sum every Sunday. Dim sum, a Cantonese term meaning "a little bit of heart," involves choosing small portions of dumplings, steamed dishes, and tarts. Hot and flavorful soup is another delicious tradition. Fresh herbs and spices highlight the cuisine of each region in sweet and sour, won ton, and specialty noodle soups served in Chinatown's restaurants. After a highly satisfying dining experience, stroll up Oxford Place, one of Chinatown's original streets, which has changed little throughout the years. Soak in the Asian-inspired architecture and admire the beauty of the Chinatown Gate that marks the entrance to this bustling neighborhood.

For a true multicultural experience, enjoy the flavors, sights, and sounds of this vibrant community.

hearty fish chowder

4   thick slices bacon, diced

2   tablespoons butter

1   large onion, diced

8   to 10 all-purpose potatoes (such as Yukon gold), peeled, cut into 1/2-inch chunks

3   cups fish, chicken or vegetable stock

2   bay leaves

>   Salt and pepper to taste

2   pounds whitefish fillets (such as haddock, codfish, or scrod), skinned, cut into large pieces

1   cup heavy cream or half-and-half

2   tablespoons finely chopped fresh thyme leaves

>   Chopped fresh parsley or chives for garnish

>   Chowder crackers

Cook the bacon in a skillet until very crisp. Drain on paper towels; set aside. Reserve the bacon drippings.

Melt the butter in a large stockpot over medium heat. Add 2 to 3 tablespoons of the reserved bacon drippings and the onion. Cook until the onion is tender but not browned. Add the potatoes, stock and bay leaves. The stock should cover the potatoes; add more stock or water if necessary. Bring to a gentle boil, covered, over medium heat. Boil for 10 minutes or until the potatoes are tender but firm. Season with salt and pepper. Reduce the heat to low.

Arrange the fish over the potatoes. Cook, covered, for 5 to 10 minutes or until the fish flakes easily. Remove from the heat. Let stand for 10 minutes. Gently stir in the cream, thyme and reserved bacon, being careful not to break up the fish too much. Let stand, covered, for 5 to 10 minutes before serving.

Remove and discard the bay leaves. To serve, spoon the fish and potatoes into bowls; top with broth. Garnish with parsley and serve with crackers.

Serves 6   *Photo on page 32*

Chowder is any variety of soup that is enriched with salt pork or fatback and thickened with flour, crushed ship biscuits, or milk. It can be made with fish, shellfish, or vegetables. Fish and clam chowders are historic New England staples.

smoked salmon chowder

To reduce the calories in creamed soups or chowders, use half-and-half, whole milk, low-fat milk, or nondairy creamer in place of heavy cream.

1	cup milk	2	(14-ounce) cans vegetable broth
1	cup water		
1	russet or Yukon gold potato, peeled, cut into quarters	1	russet or Yukon gold potato, peeled, cut into 1/2-inch cubes
5	peppercorns	1	sweet potato, peeled, cut into 1/2-inch cubes
1	bay leaf		
1	tablespoon vegetable oil	8	ounces smoked salmon, cut into bite-size pieces
1	tablespoon butter	3	tablespoons heavy cream
1	onion, chopped	2	tablespoons fresh parsley leaves, chopped
2	carrots, sliced		
1	garlic clove, minced	>	Salt and freshly ground pepper to taste
1/2	teaspoon fennel seeds		

Combine the milk, water, potato quarters, peppercorns and bay leaf in a small saucepan. Bring to a boil. Reduce the heat to low. Simmer, partially covered, for about 20 minutes or until tender. Remove from the heat and cool slightly; do not drain. Remove and discard the peppercorns and bay leaf. Process the undrained potatoes in a blender until smooth; set aside.

Heat the oil and butter in a 4-quart stockpot over medium heat. Add the onion, carrots, garlic and fennel seeds. Sauté for 8 minutes or until the vegetables are tender. Add the broth, russet potato and sweet potato. Bring to a boil. Reduce the heat to low. Simmer, covered, for 20 minutes or until the potatoes are tender but not falling apart. Gently fold in the puréed potato mixture, salmon and cream. Cook for 5 minutes to heat through. Stir in the parsley. Season with salt and pepper.

Serves 6

Uncommonly Boston — Boston's Chinatown is the third largest Chinese settlement in the United States.

new england clam chowder

WILLIAM COYNE   Executive Chef, The Union Oyster House

Chef Coyne uses only the finest local ingredients to create traditional New England dishes that reflect attention to freshness and quality. He has a reputation for serving exceptional New England seafood in a historic atmosphere where dining traditions remain unchanged.

1	quart clam juice	1/4	cup (or more) flour
1	pound potatoes, diced	2	cups (about) half-and-half, warmed
2	pounds fresh or frozen clams, diced	>	Salt and pepper to taste
2	ounces salt pork, skinned and diced	>	Tabasco sauce to taste
1	small onion, diced	>	Worcestershire sauce to taste
2	ribs celery, minced	>	Oyster or chowder crackers
1/2	cup (1 stick) butter		

Combine the clam juice and potatoes in a saucepan. Bring to a boil. Reduce the heat to low. Simmer until the potatoes are tender. Add the clams with their juices. Simmer until tender; do not overcook. Remove from the heat; set aside.

Sauté the salt pork in a pan until rendered. Add the onion and celery. Cook until tender. Add the butter. Heat until melted and cook slightly. Stir in the flour. Cook until the flour is lightly browned. If the roux is too thin, add a little more flour.

Bring the clam mixture to a boil. Stir in the roux mixture. Return to a boil. Cook until thickened, stirring constantly. Add enough of the half-and-half to reach the desired consistency. Season with salt, pepper, Tabasco sauce and Worcestershire sauce. Serve with crackers.

Serves 8

Uncommonly Boston — The Public Garden is the oldest public botanical garden in the United States.

seafood chowder

The beautiful flavor and body of a red Rhône will complement this delicious chowder without overwhelming it.

1/3	cup butter	2	cups (about) milk
1/3	cup chopped onion	1/3	cup chopped clams
2	teaspoons chopped garlic	1/3	cup chopped crab meat
1/3	cup flour	1/3	cup chopped shrimp
3	tablespoons butter	3	tablespoons lemon juice
1/3	cup chopped onion	1	tablespoon paprika
1/2	cup chopped celery	1	teaspoon Italian seasoning
1/3	cup shredded carrots	1/2	teaspoon salt
1/2	cup chopped red bliss potatoes	1/2	teaspoon black pepper
>	Salt to taste	1/4	teaspoon cayenne pepper or to taste
4	cups light cream	2	dashes of Tabasco sauce
2	cups seafood broth or fish stock	>	Fresh parsley for garnish

Melt 1/3 cup butter in a large stockpot over medium heat. Add 1/3 cup onion and garlic. Sauté until transparent. Stir in the flour. Simmer for 3 to 5 minutes, stirring frequently. Remove from the heat.

Melt 3 tablespoons butter in a medium sauté pan. Add 1/3 cup onion, the celery and carrots. Sauté until tender. Set aside.

Combine the potatoes with enough lightly salted water to cover in a saucepan. Bring to a boil. Boil for 10 minutes or until cooked through but still firm. Drain and set aside.

Bring the cream and broth to a simmer in a medium saucepan. Whisk into the flour mixture. Whisk in enough milk to reach the desired consistency. Add the clams, crab meat, shrimp, celery mixture and potatoes. Bring the chowder to a simmer. Stir in the lemon juice, paprika, Italian seasoning, 1/2 teaspoon salt, the black pepper, cayenne pepper and Tabasco sauce. Simmer for 10 minutes. Ladle into soup bowls and garnish with parsley.

Serves 8

 Uncommonly Boston — The first demonstration of ether used as an anesthetic was held in Boston in 1846 by dentist William Morton.

cream of cauliflower soup

1	head cauliflower, tough stems removed, cut into small pieces	1/2	cup low-fat sour cream
3	to 4 Yukon gold potatoes, thinly sliced	1/2	teaspoon garlic powder
4	cups chicken broth	1/4	teaspoon nutmeg
1	cup part-skim ricotta cheese	>	Salt and white pepper to taste
		>	Fresh parsley for garnish

Combine the cauliflower, potatoes and broth in a saucepan. Add enough water to cover the vegetables. Bring to a boil. Reduce the heat to low. Simmer for 15 to 20 minutes or until the vegetables are tender. Remove from the heat. Purée in a blender or food processor. Return the puréed cauliflower mixture to the saucepan. Stir in the ricotta cheese, sour cream, garlic powder, nutmeg, salt and white pepper. Serve garnished with parsley.

Serves 6 to 8

minestrone

An excellent starter course or full meal, this soup is sure to satisfy.

2	large beef shanks	1	tablespoon dried parsley
4	to 5 carrots, sliced	>	Pepper to taste
3	to 4 ribs celery, sliced	2	to 3 tablespoons olive oil
2	to 3 potatoes, sliced	2	large onions, sliced
1/2	head cabbage, shredded	6	garlic cloves, minced
1	(6-ounce) can tomato paste	1	(15-ounce) can cannellini beans (optional)
1	tablespoon salt, or to taste		

Combine the shanks and enough water to cover in a large stockpot. Stir in the carrots, celery, potatoes, cabbage, tomato paste, 1 tablespoon salt, the parsley and pepper. Heat the olive oil in a large skillet. Add the onions and garlic. Sauté until tender. Add to the stockpot. Bring to a boil. Reduce the heat to low. Simmer for 1 1/2 to 2 hours or until the meat is tender. Remove the bones from the pot. Shred the meat and return the meat to the pot. Stir in the beans and cook until heated through. Season with salt and pepper to taste.

Note: Slice and shred the vegetables in a food processor for easy preparation.

Serves 8

tarascan tomato soup

2	tablespoons vegetable oil
1	onion, chopped
3	garlic cloves, peeled, crushed
2	Anaheim chiles, seeded, chopped
1	(16-ounce) can dark red kidney beans
1	cup chopped tomatoes
4	cups vegetable stock
1	(6-ounce) can tomato paste
2	large ancho chiles, seeded, cut into thin strips
1	teaspoon oregano
1/4	teaspoon crushed red pepper
2	cups tortilla chips
1/4	cup sour cream
1/3	cup shredded Monterey Jack cheese
1/4	cup chopped scallions

Heat the oil in a large heavy pot over medium heat. Add the onion, garlic and Anaheim chiles. Sauté for 8 minutes or until the onion begins to brown.

Process the beans and tomatoes in a food processor until smooth. Add to the onion mixture. Add the stock, tomato paste, ancho chiles, oregano and crushed red pepper. Cook for 45 minutes over low heat.

Ladle the soup into bowls and top each serving with chips, sour cream, cheese and scallions.

Serves 6 to 8

Uncommonly Boston — Alexander Graham Bell first demonstrated the telephone in Boston in 1876.

zucchini soup

1 1/2   pounds zucchini, sliced (about 5 small)

  1   cup chopped onion

  2   cups chicken stock

  1   teaspoon seasoned salt

1/8   teaspoon white pepper

  1   tablespoon butter

  2   cups light cream or half-and-half

  >   Chopped parsley for garnish

Combine the zucchini, onion, stock, salt and white pepper in a saucepan. Bring to a simmer. Cook until the zucchini is tender. Add the butter and cream. Purée in batches in a blender. Serve hot or ice cold garnished with parsley.

Serves 6 to 8

A vegetable soup can be transformed into a creamed soup by puréeing it in a blender or food processor and stirring in cream or milk for extra richness.

Uncommonly Boston — Founded in 1881, the Boston Symphony Orchestra is the second oldest symphony orchestra in the country.

ham and bean pottage

Enjoy this thick, flavorful soup after raking leaves on a crisp fall day.

Soup is a great make-ahead meal. One large pot of soup can be divided into several smaller containers and frozen for use later. Most soups can remain frozen for up to one month; however, soups with potatoes or other root vegetables do not freeze well. These are best eaten within one to three days of preparation.

2	tablespoons olive oil
1	large onion, chopped
2	garlic cloves, finely chopped
4	(15-ounce) cans cannellini beans
1	(28-ounce) can diced tomatoes
2	(14-ounce) cans vegetable broth or chicken broth
2 1/2	to 3 cups diced ham
2	tablespoons chopped fresh thyme leaves
2	bay leaves
>	Pepper to taste

Heat the olive oil in a stockpot. Add the onion. Sauté until tender. Add the garlic. Sauté for 30 seconds, stirring to prevent browning. Stir in the beans, tomatoes, broth and ham and mix well. Add the thyme and bay leaves. Bring to a boil. Reduce the heat to very low. Simmer, covered, for at least 1 hour. The longer the soup simmers, the thicker it becomes. If the soup becomes too thick, add more broth or water. Remove and discard the bay leaves. Season with pepper.

Serves 8

 Uncommonly Boston — The first American subway system was opened in Boston in 1898.

split pea soup

You'll love the silky texture and smoky flavor of this all-around favorite.

1	pound split peas	1	large garlic clove
10	cups water	1	bay leaf
5	chicken bouillon cubes	1/2	teaspoon thyme
1	meaty ham bone	>	Salt and black pepper to taste
3	ribs celery with leaves, chopped	>	Crushed red pepper flakes to taste
1	onion, chopped		

Sort and rinse the split peas. Combine the split peas, water, bouillon cubes and ham bone in a large Dutch oven. Bring to a boil. Reduce the heat to low. Simmer for 3 hours. Remove from the heat; cool. Refrigerate for about 3 hours to allow the fat to solidify on the surface of the soup.

Skim the fat. Remove and reserve the ham bone. Add the celery, onion, garlic, bay leaf, thyme, salt, black pepper and red pepper to the soup. Bring to a boil. Reduce the heat to low. Simmer for 1 hour.

Remove the ham from the bone; set aside. Remove and discard the bay leaf. Purée the soup in small batches in a blender or food processor. Return the puréed soup to the Dutch oven. Stir in the ham. Simmer until heated through.

Note: For best results, use a ham bone from the butt or shank end of a baked ham.

Serves 8

Uncommonly Boston — Fannie Farmer, who authored the first cookbook aimed at training the home cook, graduated from the Boston Cooking School in 1889. Her book is still in print today.

pumpkin cider soup

A festival of fall flavors, this soup is both savory and sweet.

Delicious soup begins with a rich and flavorful stock or broth. Chicken broth is made from water, bones, and meat; chicken stock, from water and meat only. To create a perfect broth or stock, simmer over very low heat; do not boil. A long simmering time allows the liquid to reduce and the flavors to become concentrated. The broth or stock should be seasoned only after cooking is complete.

2	tablespoons butter
1	large onion, sliced
1	large Granny Smith apple, peeled, sliced
2 1/2	cups low-sodium chicken broth
1 1/4	cups apple cider
4	cups (32 ounces) canned pumpkin
1	cup half-and-half
1	teaspoon curry powder
1/2	teaspoon salt
1/4	teaspoon ground coriander
1/4	teaspoon pepper
1/2	cup sour cream for garnish
1/4	cup snipped fresh chives for garnish

Melt the butter in a large saucepan. Add the onion and apple. Sauté until tender. Purée 1/2 of the onion mixture in a food processor. Add 1/2 of the broth and 1/2 of the cider gradually, processing constantly until smooth. Pour into a saucepan. Repeat with the remaining onion mixture, broth and cider. Stir in the pumpkin, half-and-half, curry powder, salt, coriander and pepper. Cook over medium heat until heated through.

Taste and adjust the seasonings. Thin the soup with additional cider if necessary. Ladle into soup bowls and garnish each serving with a dollop of sour cream and a pinch of chives.

Serves 8

Photo on page 45

maine lobster bisque

JÉRÔME LEGRAS   Executive Chef, Aujourd'hui, Four Seasons Hotel

The cuisine of Chef Legras is built on both classic and modern French technique, as well as international experience. He has a flair for creating contemporary dishes based on the freshest regional ingredients available.

LOBSTER STOCK

2	pounds lobster heads
1	rib celery
1	carrot
1	onion
1	leek
1	bay leaf
1	thyme sprig
1	cup white wine
12	cups cold water
>	Grated zest of 1 lemon

BISQUE

2	pounds lobster heads
>	Blended oil (equal amounts of olive oil and vegetable oil)
1/2	cup brandy
1/2	carrot
1/2	onion
1	rib celery
1/2	leek
8	ounces tomato paste
4	cups lobster stock
1	thyme sprig
1	bay leaf
8	cups heavy cream
>	Salt and pepper to taste

For the stock, separate the shell from the lobster heads and remove any membranes. Rinse the heads under cold running water. Cut into quarters and pat dry. Chop the celery, carrot, onion and leek into small pieces. Combine the lobster, celery, carrot, onion, leek, bay leaf, thyme, wine, water and lemon zest in a small stockpot. Bring to a boil. Skim the foam from the top. Reduce the temperature and simmer for 45 to 60 minutes. Strain through a cheesecloth and chill over ice.

For the bisque, separate the shell from the lobster heads and remove any membranes. Rinse the heads under cold running water. Cut into quarters and pat dry. Heat a small amount of blended oil in a heavy-bottomed pan. Add the lobster and caramelize, cooking until golden and beginning to turn red, stirring frequently. Remove from the heat. Add the brandy and ignite. Return to the heat and cook until the liquid has evaporated. Spoon into a soup pot and set aside. Chop the carrot, onion, celery and leek into small pieces. Heat a small amount of blended oil in a skillet. Cook the vegetables until caramelized. Reduce the heat and add the tomato paste. Cook for 10 minutes, stirring frequently. Add to the cooked lobster. Add the lobster stock, thyme and bay leaf to the cooked lobster. Cook until reduced by 1/2. Add the cream and cook until reduced by 1/2 or until the bisque has a good lobster flavor.

Lobster Flan

8	tablespoons chopped lobster meat
1	cup heavy cream
2	eggs
2	egg yolks
1	tablespoon lobster roe
>	Salt and pepper to taste

Corn Marmalade

2	tablespoons olive oil
1	pound fresh corn kernels
1	ounce chicken stock
>	Salt and pepper to taste

Assembly

1	teaspoon butter
>	Chervil leaves or chives for garnish

Strain the bisque, pressing the solids to extract as much of the liquid as possible. Discard the solids. Press through a fine mesh sieve and discard any remaining solids. Season with salt and pepper. Chill, covered, until ready to reheat.

For the flan, preheat the oven to 350 degrees and butter four ramekins. Spoon 2 tablespoons of the lobster meat into each ramekin. Process the cream, eggs, egg yolks and roe in a blender. Season with salt and pepper. Press through a fine mesh sieve, discarding any solids. Pour over the lobster meat, filling each ramekin to just below the rim. Cover each ramekin tightly and place the ramekins in a baking pan large enough to hold all four ramekins. Add hot water to the baking pan. Bake for 10 minutes or until the flans are firm. Let stand in a warm place for 10 to 20 minutes.

For the marmalade, heat the olive oil in a heavy-bottomed pan. Add the corn and cook until enough moisture has evaporated that the corn has reduced by 1/4. Add the stock and bring to a boil. Cook until the corn is tender. Purée half the corn in a blender. Add the remaining corn and process until the mixture is chunky. Season with salt and pepper. Chill over ice.

To assemble, spoon the marmalade in a ring in the center of each of four plates. Run a knife around the inside of each ramekin and turn the flans out into the center of the plates. Heat the bisque in a saucepan. Add the butter and blend with a hand blender until frothy. Ladle into bowls and decorate with chervil leaves or chives.

Serves 4

Uncommonly Boston — Boston is known as one of the best walking cities in the United States.

tortellini soup

A simple beaujolais or a slightly more complex shiraz would complement this rustic soup.

There are two classes of soups, those made with stock and those made without stock. Soups with stock have a clear liquid base and include bouillon, consommé, brown stock soup, and white stock soup. Soups without stock have a creamy liquid base and include cream soups, bisques, chowders, and purées.

1 1/2	pounds hot sausage, casings removed
1	large onion, chopped
10	cups beef broth
1	(24-ounce) can tomato sauce
2	cups sliced carrots
2	cups sliced celery
1 1/2	cups ketchup
3/4	cup red wine (preferably merlot or cabernet sauvignon)
2	garlic cloves, minced
1	teaspoon thyme
1	teaspoon oregano
1	teaspoon basil
2	zucchini, sliced
1	large red bell pepper, chopped
1	large green bell pepper, chopped
1/3	cup fresh parsley leaves, finely chopped
1	pound fresh tortellini
>	Salt and pepper to taste
>	Freshly grated Parmesan cheese

Brown the sausage in a large soup pot, stirring until crumbly; drain. Add the onion. Sauté until tender. Stir in the broth, tomato sauce, carrots, celery, ketchup, wine, garlic, thyme, oregano and basil. Bring to a boil. Reduce the heat to low. Simmer for 30 minutes. Skim any fat from the surface of the soup. Stir in the zucchini, bell peppers and parsley. Simmer, covered, for 20 minutes.

Cook the tortellini in a separate saucepan using the package directions; drain. Stir into the soup. Season with salt and pepper. Sprinkle each serving with cheese.

Serves 12

army versus navy chili

This is a game day classic—warm, flavorful, and filling—whether you are watching Army/Navy, Harvard/Yale, or your favorite team.

2	pounds hot Italian sausage, casings removed		2	tablespoons minced garlic
1	pound ground turkey sausage		1 1/2	teaspoons salt
3	bell peppers, diced		1 1/2	teaspoons paprika
2	onions, diced		1	teaspoon oregano
1	pound sliced mushrooms		1/2	teaspoon cumin
3	(28-ounce) cans diced tomatoes		2	tablespoons flour (optional)
2	(28-ounce) cans kidney beans, drained		1	(6-ounce) can tomato paste (optional)
1	(16-ounce) can tomato sauce		1	teaspoon cayenne pepper or to taste
1	cup water		>	Shredded Cheddar cheese
1/4	cup plus 1 tablespoon chili powder		>	Sour cream
			>	Jalapeños

Brown the Italian and turkey sausages in a skillet, stirring until crumbly; drain. Combine the sausage, bell peppers, onions and mushrooms in a 4-quart slow cooker. Cook on High for 45 minutes.

Add the tomatoes, beans, tomato sauce, water, chili powder, garlic, salt, paprika, oregano and cumin. Cook on Low for 6 hours. Stir in the flour and tomato paste to reach the desired consistency. Add the cayenne pepper. Serve with cheese, sour cream and jalapeños.

Serves 10 to 12

Uncommonly Boston — Boston lays claim to the first father and son to become United States presidents. John Adams was the second president and his son, John Quincy Adams, was the sixth.

black bean chili

The rich, earthy flavors of Dunkin' Donuts Chocolate Turbo Coffee drinks will complement the spice and heat of this chili and warm up a party or family meal.

Transform this dish into individual casseroles by ladling the chili into small baking dishes and topping with crumbled corn bread or corn muffins and a mixture of Monterey Jack and Cheddar cheeses. Bake in a 350-degree oven for twenty to thirty minutes or until the cheese is bubbly and the chili is heated through.

1	tablespoon olive oil		1	tablespoon Mrs. Dash seasoning
1	pound ground turkey		1	teaspoon ground red pepper
1	large onion, chopped		1	(12-ounce) can vacuum-packed corn
2	carrots, chopped		1	cup cooked rice
2	ribs celery, chopped			
3	garlic cloves, minced		>	Shredded sharp Cheddar cheese
4	(29-ounce) cans black beans		>	Sour cream
4	cups (about) chicken broth		>	Tortilla chips
1	(6-ounce) can tomato paste			
1	tablespoon cumin, or to taste			

Heat the olive oil in a Dutch oven. Add the turkey. Cook for 5 minutes or until cooked through, stirring frequently. Add the onion, carrots, celery and garlic. Cook for 10 minutes or until the vegetables are tender. And the beans, broth, tomato paste, cumin, Mrs. Dash seasoning and red pepper. Bring to a boil. Reduce the heat to low. Simmer for 2 hours, adding more broth if the chili becomes too thick.

Stir in the corn and rice. Cook until heated through. Serve with cheese, sour cream and tortilla chips.

Serves 8

maple-roasted almond and swiss
chocolate soup

MARKUS RIPPERGER   Executive Chef, Hampshire House

Chef Ripperger brings the best of the Old World and New World together in his unique dishes. He developed this imaginative soup for a Boston chocolate tour, and it was an instant success!

1	cup slivered almonds
1	teaspoon maple syrup
4	cups milk
2	teaspoons vanilla extract
10	egg yolks
1/2	cup sugar
1	cup finely chopped bittersweet chocolate
1	cup heavy cream
1	teaspoon amaretto
1	teaspoon crème de cacao
1	teaspoon Kahlúa
>	Cookies or biscotti

Toast the almonds in a 4-quart saucepan over medium-low heat until golden brown, stirring frequently. Add the maple syrup. Stir in the milk and vanilla. Bring to a boil.

Beat the egg yolks and sugar in a bowl until slightly foamy. Whisk in the hot milk mixture gradually. Return the mixture to the saucepan. Heat just to the boiling point; do not allow the soup to boil. Cook gently until the soup coats a wooden spoon. Remove from the heat. Stir in the chocolate and cream. Add the amaretto, crème de cacao and Kahlúa. Serve with cookies.

Serves 4 to 6

citrus gazpacho

This cold soup is light, refreshing, and bright with flavor.

When you boil or steam vegetables, save the cooking water as a base for vegetable stock. To make the vegetable stock, add coarsely chopped onion, carrot, celery rib with leaves, and tomatoes to the reserved water. Simmer over very low heat for one to two hours until the flavors become concentrated. Remove the vegetables with a slotted spoon, and use the flavorful liquid in your favorite recipes that call for vegetable stock.

1	(26-ounce) jar refrigerated citrus salad, drained
1	(16-ounce) container fresh salsa
2	cups tomato juice
1 1/2	cups chopped green bell peppers
1 1/2	cups chopped seeded cucumbers
1	cup chicken broth
1	tablespoon olive oil
1/2	cup chopped fresh cilantro
>	Juice of 1 lime
1/2	to 1 cup reduced-fat sour cream
1	tablespoon honey
>	Grated zest of 1 lime
1	lime, thinly sliced, for garnish

Place the citrus salad in a large bowl. Break into small pieces with a fork. Add the salsa, tomato juice, bell peppers, cucumbers, broth and olive oil. Reserve 2 tablespoons of the cilantro. Stir the remaining cilantro and lime juice into the salsa mixture. Refrigerate, covered, for at least 2 hours to blend flavors.

Combine the sour cream, honey and lime zest in a small bowl and mix well. Refrigerate, covered, until ready to serve.

To serve, cut each lime slice into quarters. Ladle the gazpacho into individual shallow bowls. Top each serving with the sour cream mixture. Garnish with the reserved cilantro and quartered lime slices.

Serves 6

Uncommonly Boston — The historic "Community Bulletin Board" stood in the center of Chinatown until 1991. Emulating Chinese custom, it was used to post news, announcements, and information about community events.

garden vegetable gazpacho

2	large tomatoes, cut into halves		1/4	cup fresh parsley leaves, chopped
4	cups vegetable juice cocktail or tomato juice		2	tablespoons fresh cilantro leaves, chopped
1/4	cup extra-virgin olive oil		1	hothouse cucumber, peeled and chopped
1/4	cup dry red wine		1	yellow bell pepper, diced
3	tablespoons fresh lime juice		1	green bell pepper, diced
2	tablespoons red wine vinegar		2	ribs celery, chopped
1	tablespoon Worcestershire sauce		1/3	cup chopped green onions
			1/3	cup chopped red onion
2	garlic cloves, minced		>	Salt and pepper to taste
1/4	cup fresh basil leaves, chopped		1/2	avocado, sliced, for garnish
			8	ounces light sour cream, for garnish

Squeeze the tomato halves gently over a bowl to release the seeds and juices. Strain the juices, pressing to release as much juice as possible. Discard the seeds. Finely chop the tomatoes. Combine the tomatoes with their juice, vegetable juice cocktail, olive oil, wine, lime juice, vinegar, Worcestershire sauce and garlic in a large bowl. Add the basil, parsley and cilantro and mix well.

Process the cucumber, bell peppers, celery, green onions and red onion in batches in a food processor or blender to the desired texture. After each vegetable is processed, add to the tomato mixture and stir gently to combine. Season to taste with salt and pepper. Refrigerate, covered, for 1 to 2 hours or until cold. Garnish each serving with an avocado slice and a dollop of sour cream.

Serves 4 to 6

The flavors of your soup will stand out if it is served at the right temperature. Cold soups are best served cool, not ice cold. Remove the soup from the refrigerator fifteen minutes prior to serving to bring it to the proper temperature.

Boston Steak Salad

SALADS & dressings

A magnificent gift to the city, Boston's Emerald Necklace is a garden of earthly delights. Developed in the 1890s, Boston's Emerald Necklace was designed by America's first landscape architect, Frederick Law Olmsted. Olmsted was known for his passion for the outdoors and his belief that relaxing amidst nature was essential for city dwellers.

The Emerald Necklace is an expansive series of parks that stretches for seven miles and runs from Boston to Brookline. Originally, the Emerald Necklace was an uninterrupted greenway; however, as the city expanded, individual parks were formed. The Emerald Necklace took approximately eighteen years to complete and consists of six uniquely beautiful parks, each with its own history.

Boston Common and the Public Garden are located in the heart of the city on seventy-five acres. Boston Common was communal land used for the grazing of livestock and later became a camping ground for British troops. The government took over the land in 1634 and created the nation's first public park. Today, Boston Common is alive with activity from ice skating on the Frog Pond to picnics under the shady trees.

The Public Garden is located directly across from Boston Common and boasts flower beds that are constantly in bloom. Designed in 1839 to reflect a French style, the Public Garden was the first botanical garden in the United States. The willow-lined pond of the Public Garden is home to Boston's famous swan boats. In the spring, families bring their children to ride the swan boats and watch for newly hatched ducklings.

The Commonwealth Mall was patterned after the French boulevards. Its wide, tree-lined pathway is framed on both sides by incredible brownstone homes and provides a beautiful setting for strolling, jogging, or sitting.

The Back Bay Fens beautified the once-odorous and wet marshland of the western portion of the city. Located near the Museum of Fine Arts and Isabella Stewart Gardner Museum, the Fens is alive with museum-goers and art students. This area is also home to an amazing Olmsted-designed rose garden boasting more than one hundred species of roses.

The Riverway Park is located at the intersection of Boston and Brookline. It is 100 percent man-made and is the narrowest part of the Necklace. Riverway Park follows the path of the Muddy River. Nearby Olmsted Park, Arnold Arboretum, and Franklin Park are all much larger. Jamaica Park, considered to be the jewel of the Emerald Necklace, contains Jamaica Pond, the largest body of pure water in Boston. The Arnold Arboretum covers 265 acres and is a center for horticulture. Franklin Park, the largest element of the Emerald Necklace, has 520 acres of trails, grassland, and ponds.

The Emerald Necklace provides a green oasis for the citizens of Boston. Pack a picnic, stroll through the greenway, and enjoy the natural beauty hidden in the city.

boston steak salad

STEAK

3/4	cup soy sauce
1/2	cup vegetable oil
1/4	cup rice wine vinegar
2	tablespoons honey
3	garlic cloves, crushed
1/2	teaspoon rosemary
3	pounds flank steak or London broil

SALAD

2	(10-ounce) packages julienned carrots
3	(8-ounce) cans water chestnuts, drained, sliced
4	cups chopped celery
1	pound sugar snap peas, blanched
3	red bell peppers, sliced
1	red onion, sliced

DRESSING

1/2	cup olive oil
1/2	cup soy sauce
1/4	cup rice wine vinegar
3	tablespoons honey
3	garlic cloves, minced
1/2	teaspoon sesame oil

ASSEMBLY

1	head Boston or Bibb lettuce

For the steak, combine the soy sauce, oil, vinegar, honey, garlic and rosemary in a bowl. Place the flank steak in a shallow dish. Pour the marinade over the steak. Marinate, covered, in the refrigerator for 3 to 12 hours. Remove the steak from the marinade; discard the marinade. Grill the steak to desired doneness. Carve across the grain into very thin slices. Cut the slices into bite-size pieces.

For the salad, combine the steak, carrots, water chestnuts, celery, peas, bell peppers and onion in a large bowl.

For the dressing, whisk the olive oil, soy sauce, vinegar, honey, garlic and sesame oil in a bowl. Pour over the salad and toss to coat.

To assemble, arrange the lettuce leaves on six to eight salad plates. Spoon the steak mixture evenly over the leaves and serve.

Serves 6 to 8

Photo on page 54

There are four varieties of lettuce: butterhead, such as Boston and Bibb, has loose heads, grassy leaves, and a buttery, mild texture and flavor; looseleaf, such as red leaf and green leaf, doesn't form lettuce heads, but has leaves that are joined at the stem; romaine, or cos, has loaf-shaped heads with darker outer leaves, a crisp texture, and strong taste; crisphead, such as iceberg, has tightly packed, round heads with pale-colored leaves, a mild flavor, and crisp texture. Crisphead is the least nutritious of the salad greens.

Uncommonly Boston — In 1634, the Boston Common became the first public park in America.

salad dressing

1	cup red wine vinegar	2	cups vegetable oil
1/2	cup sugar	1/2	onion, minced
1 1/2	teaspoons dry mustard	1/2	cup chopped macadamia nuts
1	teaspoon salt	2	tablespoons papaya seeds

Combine the vinegar, sugar, dry mustard and salt in a blender. Add the oil gradually, processing constantly at high speed until smooth. Pour into a serving bowl.

Combine the onion, macadamia nuts and papaya seeds in a blender and process until mixed. Stir into the dressing mixture. Refrigerate, covered, for several hours. Serve over tossed greens.

Serves 8 to 10

arugula salad

1	pound arugula	3/4	teaspoon garlic powder
>	Parmigiano-Reggiano cheese	>	Pinch of salt
1/4	cup balsamic vinegar, or to taste	>	Large pinch of pepper
1	tablespoon Dijon mustard	1/4	cup olive oil
3/4	teaspoon sugar		

Wash and dry the arugula. Place in a wide bowl. Shave the cheese in long thin strips over the top of the arugula using a vegetable peeler.

Combine the vinegar, Dijon mustard, sugar, garlic powder, salt and pepper in a bowl. Whisk in the olive oil gradually and continue whisking until the dressing emulsifies. Drizzle a desired amount over the salad.

Serves 6 to 8

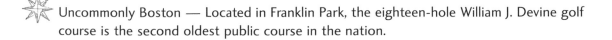

Uncommonly Boston — Located in Franklin Park, the eighteen-hole William J. Devine golf course is the second oldest public course in the nation.

feta, pear and watercress salad

The salty feta cheese, sweet pears, and peppery greens make this salad a success.

1 1/2	cups tightly packed torn red leaf lettuce	1	teaspoon water
1/2	cup tightly packed trimmed watercress	1	teaspoon walnut oil or vegetable oil
1/2	cup thinly sliced red pear	1	teaspoon Dijon mustard
2	tablespoons crumbled feta cheese	>	Dash of garlic powder
1	tablespoon balsamic vinegar	>	Dash of oregano

Wash and dry the lettuce and watercress. Divide the lettuce, watercress and pear evenly between two salad plates. Sprinkle with the cheese.

Combine the vinegar, water, walnut oil, Dijon mustard, garlic powder and oregano in a small bowl. Drizzle evenly over the salads.

Serves 2

field greens with cranberries
and walnuts

Try a spicy Alsatian white wine to complement this harvest-inspired salad.

SALAD

6	to 8 cups mixed field greens, washed
3/4	cup dried cranberries
1/2	cup chopped walnuts

DRESSING

1/4	cup olive oil
2	tablespoons balsamic vinegar
1	teaspoon herbes de Provence
1	teaspoon toasted sesame seeds
1/2	teaspoon kosher salt
1/2	teaspoon pepper

For the salad, combine the field greens, dried cranberries and walnuts in a large salad bowl.

For the dressing, whisk the olive oil, vinegar, herbes de Provence, sesame seeds, salt and pepper in a small bowl. Toss the dressing with the salad. Serve immediately.

Serves 6

curry salad

When choosing spinach for a salad, look for crisp, bright-green leaves with no dark or yellow patches. A thin, flexible stem indicates a tender, young plant that will be perfect used raw in salad. Stems that are thicker and more fibrous usually indicate an older, tougher plant that is best eaten cooked.

10	ounces fresh spinach	1/4	cup white wine vinegar
1 1/2	cups diced apples	1/4	cup olive oil
1/2	cup golden raisins, or to taste	2	tablespoons mango chutney
1/2	cup crushed unsalted dry-roasted peanuts	1 1/2	teaspoons curry powder
		1	teaspoon dry mustard
2	to 3 tablespoons chopped green onions	1/2	teaspoon sugar
		1/2	teaspoon salt

Place the spinach, apples, raisins, peanuts and green onions in a large bowl; toss to combine. Whisk the vinegar, olive oil, chutney, curry powder, dry mustard, sugar and salt in a bowl. Or, place in a jar, cover tightly and shake well. Pour the dressing over the spinach mixture and toss to coat.

Serves 4

german coleslaw

1	head of green or purple cabbage, shredded, or 1 (12-ounce) package shredded cabbage	1	cup white vinegar
		2	teaspoons sugar
		1	teaspoon dry mustard
1	large white onion, coarsely chopped (about 1 1/2 cups)	3/4	cup vegetable oil
		1	teaspoon salt
1	cup sugar	1	teaspoon celery seeds

Combine the cabbage, onion and 1 cup sugar in a large bowl. Combine the vinegar, 2 teaspoons sugar, the dry mustard, oil, salt and celery seeds in a saucepan. Bring to a boil. Pour over the cabbage mixture and toss to combine. Chill for 4 to 5 hours. May be made a few days in advance and chilled.

Serves 6

strawberry-spinach salad

1   to 1 1/2 pounds fresh baby spinach, thoroughly washed

1   pint strawberries, sliced

1   cup (4 ounces) shredded Cheddar cheese

1/2   cup chopped walnuts

1   cup olive oil or vegetable oil

3/4   cup sugar

1/2   cup red wine vinegar

2   garlic cloves, minced

1/2   teaspoon salt

1/4   teaspoon pepper

>   Dash of paprika

Combine the spinach, strawberries, cheese and walnuts in a large bowl. Whisk the olive oil, sugar, vinegar, garlic, salt, pepper and paprika in a bowl. Pour the desired amount of dressing over the salad and toss to coat. You will not need all of the dressing; increase the amounts of the salad ingredients to use all the dressing.

Serves 4 to 6

sweet spinach salad

This earthy and sweet salad is delicious for lunch or dinner.

1   (10- or 16-ounce) package fresh spinach

10   slices bacon, crisp-cooked, crumbled

1   (8-ounce) can sliced water chestnuts, drained, chopped

4   or 5 hard-cooked eggs, chopped

4   scallions, green parts only, chopped

1   cup canola oil

1/2   cup granulated sugar

1/3   cup cider vinegar

1/4   cup packed light brown sugar

1/4   cup ketchup

1   small onion, cut into chunks

1   tablespoon Worcestershire sauce

>   Dash of salt

For the salad, wash and dry the spinach. Remove and discard the stems. Tear the leaves into bite-size pieces. Place in a large bowl. Add the bacon, water chestnuts, hard-cooked eggs and scallions.

For the dressing, combine the canola oil, granulated sugar, vinegar, brown sugar, ketchup, onion, Worcestershire sauce and salt in a blender and process at high speed until smooth. Pour the desired amount of dressing over the salad and toss to coat.

Serves 6

warm goat cheese salad

For an elegant first course, wash the greens and make the dressing ahead of time, and then bake the goat cheese just before serving.

Bosc pears are brown skinned and do not change color when ripe. They have distinctive long, tapering necks and fat bottoms. Their flesh is sweet and highly aromatic. They are delicious raw or cooked and ideal for slicing into salads, poaching, and baking.

DRESSING

- 2 tablespoons fresh lemon juice
- 2 tablespoons red wine vinegar
- 1/2 teaspoon Dijon mustard
- 1/4 teaspoon sugar
- 3 tablespoons extra-virgin olive oil
- 3 tablespoons walnut oil
- > Salt and freshly ground pepper to taste

GOAT CHEESE

- 1/2 cup hazelnuts, finely chopped
- 1/2 cup bread crumbs
- 8 ounces goat cheese, cut into 8 slices
- 1/4 cup extra-virgin olive oil

SALAD

- 1 head Boston lettuce, torn into bite-size pieces
- 1 head red leaf lettuce, torn into bite-size pieces
- 1 Bosc pear, thinly sliced
- 1/3 cup sliced almonds, lightly toasted

For the dressing, combine the lemon juice, vinegar, Dijon mustard and sugar in a small bowl. Add the olive oil and walnut oil in a fine stream, whisking constantly. Season with salt and pepper.

For the goat cheese, combine the hazelnuts and bread crumbs in a small bowl. Coat the cheese slices with olive oil and then coat in the bread crumb mixture. Place on an oiled baking sheet. Bake at 400 degrees for 10 to 15 minutes or until lightly browned.

For the salad, place the Boston lettuce, leaf lettuce, pear and almonds in a large bowl. Add the dressing and toss gently. Serve on individual plates; top each with a goat cheese round.

Serves 8

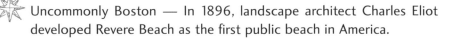

Uncommonly Boston — In 1896, landscape architect Charles Eliot developed Revere Beach as the first public beach in America.

tuscan bean insalata

2 cups canned cannellini beans, rinsed, well drained

1 small red bell pepper, cut into bite-size pieces

1/2 small red onion, cut into bite-size pieces

1/2 cup kalamata olives, coarsely chopped

1/2 cup chopped oil-pack sun-dried tomatoes

3 garlic cloves, minced

1/4 cup fresh lemon juice

1/4 cup olive oil

> Salt and pepper to taste

4 to 5 lettuce leaves for garnish

1/4 cup Vermont goat cheese, finely crumbled

4 to 5 fresh basil leaves, julienned

The cannellini bean is a traditional white Italian bean that is also known as a white kidney bean. It has a very smooth texture, a nutty flavor, and is widely used in Italian cuisine.

Combine the beans, bell pepper, onion, olives, sun-dried tomatoes and garlic in a large mixing bowl. Drizzle with the lemon juice and olive oil; toss gently to coat. Season lightly with salt and pepper. Refrigerate, covered, for at least 30 minutes to blend flavors.

Remove the salad from the refrigerator at least 10 minutes before serving. This salad is best when served at room temperature. Arrange the lettuce leaves on a serving platter. Spoon the salad over the lettuce. Top with the cheese and basil.

Serves 8

Uncommonly Boston — It took nearly twenty years for the six public parks that are now known as the "Emerald Necklace" to be completed.

melon with feta, red onion
and pine nuts

A late-harvest riesling balances nicely with the sweet, salty, and savory flavors of this salad.

2	red onions, sliced 1/4 inch thick	2	tablespoons fresh lime juice
1	tablespoon vegetable oil	>	Salt and pepper to taste
2	cantaloupes	1/2	cup crumbled feta cheese
1	honeydew melon	1/4	cup pine nuts, toasted
1/4	cup chopped fresh mint leaves		

Cook the onions in the oil in a large skillet over medium heat until softened, stirring occasionally. Remove from the heat and let stand until cool. Cut a slice from the top and bottom of each melon. Stand a melon on a cutting board with a cut side down. Remove the rind, cutting from the top to the bottom. Cut the melon into 3/4-inch chunks, discarding the seeds. Place in a bowl. Repeat with the remaining melons. Add the mint, lime juice, salt and pepper to the melons and toss to combine. Spoon onto a platter. Top with the cooked onions. Sprinkle with the feta cheese and pine nuts. Toss just before serving.

Serves 8

Photo on page 65

tomato salad

6	tomatoes, at room temperature	1	teaspoon finely chopped fresh basil
1	red onion	3/4	teaspoon garlic powder
1/2	cup balsamic vinegar	>	Pinch of salt
1	teaspoon sugar	>	Large pinch of pepper
1	teaspoon finely chopped fresh oregano	1/2	cup olive oil

Slice the tomatoes into thin wedges and place in a large bowl. Slice the onion into very thin slices and cut each slice in half. Add to the tomatoes. Pour the vinegar into a small bowl. Add the sugar, oregano, basil, garlic powder, salt and pepper. Whisk in the olive oil gradually and continue whisking until the mixture emulsifies. Pour over the tomatoes and onion. Let stand at room temperature for 1 hour or longer.

Serves 6 to 8

vegetarian caviar

This salad is a colorful and flavorful alternative for picnics and cookouts.

2	(16-ounce) cans dark red kidney beans, drained	1/4	cup chopped red onion
1	(16-ounce) can chick-peas, drained	1/2	to 1 jalapeño chile, minced
1	(16-ounce) can black-eyed peas, drained (optional)	1/2	to 2/3 cup raisins
2	large tomatoes, chopped	1/2	cup seasoned rice vinegar
2	ribs celery, chopped	1/3	cup fresh cilantro leaves, chopped
1	yellow bell pepper, diced	2	tablespoons olive oil
1/4	cup chopped green onions	1	large garlic clove, minced
		1/4	teaspoon kosher salt

Combine the beans, chick-peas and black-eyed peas in a large bowl. Combine the tomatoes, celery, bell pepper, green onions, red onion, jalapeño chile and raisins in a small bowl. Add to the beans and mix gently with a rubber spatula.

Whisk the vinegar, cilantro, olive oil, garlic and salt in a small bowl. Pour 1/2 of the dressing over the bean mixture and mix gently. Refrigerate, tightly covered, for several hours to allow the flavors to blend. Serve chilled. Reserve the remaining dressing for another use.

Serves 10 to 12

Uncommonly Boston — The Arnold Arboretum is North America's first public arboretum.

roquefort flans with duck salad

DEBORAH HUGHES   Chef/Owner, Upstairs on the Square
MARY-CATHERINE DEIBEL   Owner/Host, Upstairs on the Square

These owner-operators are known for providing a memorable dining experience. Their magnificent menus feature dishes that are beautifully presented and highlight the best seasonal and local ingredients. The glamorously funky décor complements the casual haute cuisine offered in their Monday Club Bar and sunny Zebra Room, as well as the classic fine dining offered in their Soirée Room.

ROQUEFORT FLANS

2	cups (or less) Roquefort cheese
16	ounces cream cheese, softened
2	cups sour cream
6	egg yolks
>	Dash of lemon juice
>	Fresh thyme leaves to taste
>	Freshly cracked pepper to taste
1/2	cup heavy cream
2	tablespoons clarified butter
1/4	cup fine bread crumbs

DRESSING AND SALAD

2	cups extra-virgin olive oil
2/3	cup raspberry vinegar
3	tablespoons honey

2	garlic cloves, minced
>	Finely chopped fresh rosemary leaves to taste
>	Coarse salt and freshly ground pepper to taste
4	duck breasts, seared, sautéed to rare
8	cups (about) fresh bitter organic greens
2	cups cooked white beans or cranberry beans
1	cup pitted kalamata olives
1	cup fresh orange sections, membranes removed, each section cut into halves
1/2	cup finely diced red onion
1/2	cup crumbled crisp-cooked pancetta or Cobb bacon
>	Fresh sage leaves, deep-fried in clarified butter, lightly salted, for garnish

For the Roquefort flans, pulse the Roquefort cheese in a food processor until crumbly. Add the next 6 ingredients and process until smooth. Stir in the heavy cream. Lightly grease eight 6-ounce ramekins with the clarified butter; dust with the bread crumbs. Pour the flan mixture evenly into the prepared ramekins. Place the ramekins in a water bath. Bake at 350 degrees for 1 hour or until set. Cool to room temperature.

For the dressing and salad, whisk the first 7 ingredients in a bowl and set aside. Carve the duck breasts into thin slices. Toss the greens with enough dressing to coat lightly. Arrange the greens on 10-inch plates. Top evenly with the beans, olives, oranges, onion and pancetta. Remove the flans from the ramekins. Place in the center of the greens. Surround the flans with fans of sliced duck breast. Garnish with sage leaves.

Serves 4 as a main course, 8 as a first course

Yogurt Waffles with Tipsy Strawberries

BRUNCH
& breads

Beacon Hill is one of Boston's oldest and most picturesque neighborhoods. It is a neighborhood meant for walking. Whether you are a history enthusiast, a student of architecture, or simply an admirer of beautiful things, you will enjoy a ramble on the hill. Located in downtown Boston, this quaint village covers approximately one square mile and is home to 10,000 people.

The neighborhood was originally pastureland owned by famed painter John Singleton Copley. Beginning in the 1790s and continuing through the 1800s, lavish homes were built on the south side of the hill for Boston's most distinguished citizens, the Brahmins. The south side of the hill overlooks Beacon Street and America's oldest urban park, Boston Common. Beacon Street is also the home to the Bull & Finch pub. Designed by the famed Boston architect Charles Bullfinch, the pub was the model for the friendly neighborhood bar in the television show *Cheers.*

The north side of the hill had more humble origins. The winding streets, hidden doorways, and narrow alleyways were home to tradesmen, sailors, and former slaves. The north side of the hill also overlooks Cambridge Street, which is the home to restaurants, bars, and Massachusetts General Hospital, one of the country's most renowned medical facilities.

The architecture of Beacon Hill remains unchanged, with its original homes, carriage houses, and stables. Most of Beacon Hill's streets are tree-lined and still lit with gas lanterns. Red brick sidewalks wind through the stunning architecture of this small neighborhood, where hidden squares and gardens peek out from every turn. The majestic gold-domed State House, originally installed by Paul Revere, sits atop Beacon Hill. The top of the hill is also the starting point for Boston's famous Freedom Trail. Willow Street dips through the middle of the hill. Entirely paved of cobblestone and lined with its original homes, Willow Street is arguably the most photographed street in America.

Charles Street runs through the center of Beacon Hill, parallel to the Charles River. As quaint as the residential streets, Charles Street serves as the commercial hub of Beacon Hill. Known for its specialty markets and wine stores, the long, meandering street is flanked by some of the best restaurants, boutiques, and antique shops in Boston. Brunch is best enjoyed in one of Charles Street's aromatic cafes, bakeries, or coffee shops, where outdoor seating is always at a premium.

Visit Beacon Hill and soak in the history of the neighborhood while sharing the pleasure of brunch with friends or family.

yogurt waffles

2	egg whites	1	cup flour
2	egg yolks	1	tablespoon sugar
8	ounces plain yogurt	1	teaspoon baking powder
3	tablespoons butter, melted	1/2	teaspoon baking soda
2	tablespoons water	1/4	teaspoon salt

Beat the egg whites in a medium mixing bowl until stiff peaks form; set aside.

Beat the egg yolks in a large mixing bowl until thick. Stir in the yogurt, butter and water. Sift the flour, sugar, baking powder, baking soda and salt into the egg yolk mixture. Beat until smooth. Fold in the egg whites gently.

Cook in a waffle iron until crisp using the manufacturer's instructions.

Serves 2   *Photo on page 68*

Photo on page 68

tipsy strawberries

1/3	cup packed dark brown sugar	1	teaspoon maple syrup
		1	teaspoon vanilla extract
1/3	cup bourbon	1 1/2	pints strawberries, sliced or
1	teaspoon lemon juice		cut into quarters

Combine the brown sugar, bourbon, lemon juice, maple syrup and vanilla in a large bowl and mix well. Add the strawberries and mix well to coat. Refrigerate, covered, for 8 to 12 hours.

Serve cold over waffles or with pound cake or vanilla ice cream.

Serves 6   *Photo on page 68*

Photo on page 68

To remove waffles from the waffle iron without damaging them, insert a wooden skewer into each side of the waffle and lift gently. This prevents any tears and allows you to serve perfect waffles every time.

carriage house pancakes

3	cups flour	1/3	cup plain yogurt or vanilla yogurt
3	tablespoons sugar	2	eggs, beaten
2 1/2	teaspoons baking soda	1	teaspoon vanilla extract
1	teaspoon baking powder	>	Butter
1/4	teaspoon salt (optional)	>	Maple syrup
2 1/2	cups milk		

Sift the flour, sugar, baking soda, baking powder and salt into a large mixing bowl; set aside.

Measure the milk in a 4-cup measuring cup. Add the yogurt and eggs and mix well. Stir in the vanilla. Make a well in the center of the flour mixture. Pour all but 1/2 cup of the milk mixture into the well. Stir with a rubber spatula for five to six quick strokes to combine. Add the remaining milk mixture and mix well. The batter should be the consistency of sour cream.

Pour 1/3 cup batter at a time onto a hot, lightly greased griddle. Cook until bubbles appear on the surface and the underside is golden brown. Turn the pancake. Cook for 1 minute or until golden brown. Serve with butter and maple syrup.

Serves 6

 Uncommonly Boston — The large golden dome of the State House, a Boston landmark since it was gilded in 1861, was painted black during the Second World War.

baked french toast

A weekend breakfast or brunch feels decadent and luxurious when you pair Dunkin' Donuts creamy Cinnamon Latte with this delicious baked French toast.

1 loaf French bread or challah, cut into cubes	1/4 cup maple syrup
8 ounces cream cheese, cut into cubes	3 to 5 teaspoons butter, melted
1/2 cup packed brown sugar	1 teaspoon brown sugar
2 1/2 cups milk	1/4 teaspoon cinnamon
8 eggs, beaten	> Maple syrup, warmed

Place 1/2 of the bread cubes in the bottom of a greased 9×13-inch baking pan. Top with the cream cheese, 1/2 cup brown sugar and the remaining bread cubes.

Combine the milk, eggs, 1/4 cup maple syrup and the butter in a bowl. Pour over the bread. Press the bread down into the liquid. Combine 1 teaspoon brown sugar and the cinnamon in a small bowl and mix well. Sprinkle over the top. Cover with plastic wrap. Refrigerate for 8 to 12 hours.

Bake, uncovered, at 325 degrees for 40 to 45 minutes or until golden brown. Serve with warm maple syrup.

Serves 4 to 6

vegetarian yorkshire pudding

1 cup flour, sifted	2 eggs
1 cup milk	1/2 teaspoon salt

Beat the flour, milk, eggs and salt in a bowl with a fork. Divide the batter evenly among twelve greased muffin cups. Bake at 425 degrees for 20 to 30 minutes or until browned on top. Serve warm.

Serves 12

parker house rolls

GERRY TICE   Executive Chef, Parker's Restaurant, Parker House Hotel

6	cups flour	2	cups hot water (120 to 130 degrees)
1/2	cup sugar	1	egg
2	envelopes dry yeast	1/2	cup (1 stick) butter or margarine, softened
2	teaspoons salt		
1/2	cup (1 stick) butter or margarine, softened		

Combine 2 1/4 cups of the flour, the sugar, yeast and salt in a large mixing bowl. Add 1/2 cup butter. Gradually add the hot water, beating with a mixer at low speed. Add the egg. Beat at medium speed for 2 minutes, scraping the bowl with a rubber spatula. Beat in 3/4 cup of the flour or enough to make a thick batter. Beat for 2 minutes longer, scraping the bowl occasionally. Stir in enough of the remaining flour (about 2 1/2 cups) with a spoon to make a soft dough.

Knead the dough on a lightly floured surface for 10 minutes or until smooth and elastic, adding the remaining flour while kneading. Shape the dough into a ball. Place in a large greased bowl, turning to coat the surface. Let rise, covered, in a warm place for 1 1/2 hours or until doubled in bulk. Punch the dough down. Knead gently on a lightly floured surface to make a smooth ball. Invert the bowl over the dough and let rest for 15 minutes.

Melt 1/2 cup butter in an 11×17-inch baking sheet over low heat. Tilt the pan to evenly cover the bottom with butter. Roll the dough 1/2 inch thick on a lightly floured surface with a floured rolling pin. Cut with a floured 2 3/4-inch biscuit cutter. Dip both sides of each dough circle into the melted butter in the pan; fold in half. Arrange in rows in the baking sheet so the rolls are almost touching. Let rise, covered, for about 40 minutes or until doubled in bulk. Bake at 400 degrees for 15 to 18 minutes or until browned.

Serves 42

Uncommonly Boston — Established in Boston in 1839, Tremont Temple was the first fully integrated church in America.

irish soda bread

2	cups flour	1/2	teaspoon salt
2	tablespoons sugar	3	tablespoons butter
2	teaspoons baking powder	1	cup raisins
1/2	teaspoon baking soda	1	cup buttermilk

Sift the flour, sugar, baking powder, baking soda and salt into a bowl. Cut in the butter until crumbly. Stir in the raisins. Add the buttermilk and stir to combine. The dough will be sticky.

Spread the dough in a greased 8- or 9-inch cast-iron skillet. Bake at 350 degrees for 35 minutes or until golden brown. Serve warm with butter.

Serves 8 to 10

Irish soda bread is a classic offering in the Boston area. The primary ingredients include buttermilk, flour, raisins, baking soda, and sugar. Enjoy it with a cup of tea at any time of the day or night. It's delicious toasted with butter or torn from a hot bread round.

brahmin banana bread

1/2	cup shortening	1/2	cup rolled oats
1	cup sugar	1/2	cup fresh blueberries (optional)
2	eggs		
1	cup mashed bananas	1	teaspoon baking soda
1 1/2	cups flour	1/4	teaspoon salt

Cream the shortening in a mixing bowl. Add the sugar gradually, beating until light and fluffy. Add the eggs one at a time, beating well after each addition. Stir in the bananas. Combine the flour, oats, blueberries, baking soda and salt in a bowl. Add to the creamed mixture and stir until the dry ingredients are moistened. Pour into a greased 5×9-inch loaf pan. Bake at 350 degrees for 55 minutes or until the bread tests done. Cool in the pan for 10 minutes. Remove to a wire rack to cool completely.

Serves 12

cranberry-oat scones

2 1/4 cups flour

1/2 cup rolled oats

7 tablespoons sugar

3/4 teaspoon baking powder

3/4 teaspoon baking soda

1/4 teaspoon salt

3/4 cup (1 1/2 sticks) butter, cut into 1/4-inch pieces

1/2 cup dried cranberries

> Grated zest of 1 orange

3/4 cup buttermilk

1/4 cup (about) milk

3 tablespoons sugar

Combine the flour, oats, 7 tablespoons sugar, the baking powder, baking soda and salt in a mixing bowl. Cut in the butter until crumbly. Stir in the cranberries and orange zest. Add the buttermilk and stir gently with a wooden spoon until a dough forms; do not overmix.

Pat the dough out to about a 2-inch-thick round on a lightly floured surface. Cut into eight equal-size wedges. Place on a nonstick baking sheet or parchment-lined baking sheet. Brush the tops with milk; lightly sprinkle with 3 tablespoons sugar. Bake at 375 degrees for 20 to 23 minutes or until the edges are lightly browned. Serve warm.

Serves 8

Photo on page 76

Create a substitute for buttermilk by adding one tablespoon lemon juice to one cup room-temperature whole milk and letting the mixture stand for five minutes. The milk will sour and can be used in place of buttermilk in any recipe.

Uncommonly Boston — The first abolitionist newspaper, *The Liberator*, was published in Boston by William Lloyd Garrison in 1831.

donegal irish scones

3	cups flour	1	teaspoon salt
1	cup raisins	1	egg
3/4	cup sugar	>	Milk
2	teaspoons baking powder	1/2	cup (1 stick) butter, melted

Combine the flour, raisins, sugar, baking powder and salt in a bowl. Beat the egg in a liquid measuring cup. Add enough milk to the egg to measure 1 cup. Make a well in the center of the dry ingredients. Pour the milk mixture and butter into the well. Stir to form a lumpy, sticky dough.

Shape the dough with your hands into twelve scones. Place on a greased baking sheet. Bake at 300 degrees for 30 to 45 minutes or until golden brown and a wooden pick inserted into the center comes out clean.

Serves 12

fall brunch pumpkin muffins

Moist, spicy, and flavorful, these muffins taste and smell delectable.

2	cups flour	1	cup vegetable oil
2	cups sugar	3	eggs, lightly beaten
2 1/2	teaspoons cinnamon	2	teaspoons vanilla extract
2	teaspoons baking soda	1 1/2	cups canned pumpkin
2	teaspoons ground ginger	1	cup shredded coconut
1	teaspoon salt	1	cup chopped walnuts
1	teaspoon allspice	3/4	cup canned crushed pineapple
1	teaspoon grated gingerroot		

Combine the flour, sugar, cinnamon, baking soda, ground ginger, salt, allspice and gingerroot in a large bowl. Add the oil, eggs and vanilla and mix well. Fold in the pumpkin, coconut, walnuts and pineapple. Fill twenty-four paper-lined muffin cups 3/4 full. Bake at 350 degrees for 15 to 20 minutes or until a wooden pick inserted into the center comes out clean. Remove to a wire rack to cool.

Serves 24

jordan marsh
blueberry muffins

These famous muffins were baked daily and sold in the bakery at Jordan Marsh Department Store, which operated in Boston from 1851 until 1996.

1/2	cup (1 stick) butter, softened
1 1/4	cups granulated sugar
2	eggs
1	teaspoon vanilla extract
2	cups flour
2	teaspoons baking powder
1/2	teaspoon salt
1/2	cup milk
2 1/2	cups fresh or frozen blueberries
>	Coarse sugar for topping

Cream the butter and granulated sugar in a mixing bowl until light and fluffy. Add the eggs and vanilla and mix well. Sift the flour, baking powder and salt together. Add to the creamed mixture alternately with the milk, mixing after each addition. Fold in the blueberries. Refrigerate, covered, for 30 minutes.

Spoon the batter into twelve paper-lined muffin cups. Sprinkle with coarse sugar. Bake at 375 degrees for 20 to 25 minutes or until the muffins test done. Cool in the pan.

Serves 12

When choosing blueberries for baking or serving fresh, select smooth-skinned berries that are firm, dry, and plump. Berries should be deep purple-blue to blue-black; reddish berries aren't ripe but can be used in cooking.

Uncommonly Boston — The first American Christmas card was printed by Louis Prang in Boston in 1875.

apricot-almond coffee cake

This coffee cake is buttery, light, and delicious. The fruity taste lets it stand alone for breakfast.

1	cup (2 sticks) butter, softened	1	teaspoon baking powder
2	cups sugar	1/4	teaspoon salt
2	eggs	1	cup plus 3 tablespoons slivered almonds
1	cup sour cream		
1	teaspoon almond extract	1	(10-ounce) jar apricot preserves
2	cups flour		

Cream the butter and sugar in a mixing bowl until light and fluffy. Beat in the eggs one at a time. Fold in the sour cream and almond extract. Sift the flour, baking powder and salt together. Fold into the creamed mixture. Pour 1/3 of the batter into a greased and floured tube pan. Top with 1/2 cup of the almonds and 1/2 of the preserves. Repeat the layers. Top with the remaining 1/3 of the batter. Sprinkle with 3 tablespoons almonds. Bake at 350 degrees for 50 to 55 minutes or until the cake tests done. Cool in the pan for 10 minutes. Run a knife around the inside of the pan to loosen the cake. Invert onto a serving plate.

Serves 12

norwegian apple cake

1	cup chopped peeled apples, such as Granny Smith or Empire	1/2	cup flour
1/2	cup chopped walnuts	1	teaspoon baking powder
1/2	teaspoon vanilla extract	1	egg, beaten
3/4	cup sugar	3	tablespoons cinnamon-sugar

Combine the apples, walnuts and vanilla in a bowl and toss to combine. Sprinkle evenly over the bottom of a buttered 9-inch pan. Combine the sugar, flour and baking powder in a separate bowl and mix well. Add the egg and mix well. Spoon over the apple mixture; the batter will not completely cover the apple mixture. Sprinkle the cinnamon-sugar over the top. Bake at 350 degrees for 30 minutes or until the cake tests done. Invert onto a plate and serve warm.

Serves 6

cape cod cran-blueberry cake

CAKE

2	cups flour
1	cup sugar
1	tablespoon baking powder
3/4	teaspoon salt
1/2	cup (1 stick) butter or margarine
1	cup milk
2	eggs, beaten
1	teaspoon vanilla extract

1/2	cup blueberries
1/2	cup cranberries

TOPPING

1/2	cup chopped walnuts
1/3	cup granulated sugar
1/3	cup packed brown sugar
1	tablespoon butter, melted
2	teaspoons cinnamon

For the cake, combine the flour, sugar, baking powder and salt in a large bowl. Cut in the butter until crumbly. Make a well in the center of the dry ingredients. Pour the milk, eggs and vanilla into the well. Stir just until the dry ingredients are moistened. Pour into a greased 9×13-inch cake pan. Scatter the blueberries and cranberries over the batter.

For the topping, combine the walnuts, granulated sugar, brown sugar, butter and cinnamon in a small bowl. Sprinkle evenly over the batter. Bake at 350 degrees for 30 to 45 minutes or until a wooden pick inserted into the center of the cake comes out clean.

Serves 12

eggs with crab and scallops

12	ounces scallops, minced
6	ounces lump crab meat
1	plum tomato, diced
3	scallions, chopped
1	teaspoon dill weed
1	teaspoon lemon juice

>	Dash of hot red pepper sauce
2	tablespoons butter or margarine
4	eggs, beaten
1/3	cup sour cream
>	Toast or hot cooked grits

Combine the first 7 ingredients in a bowl. Melt the butter in a large skillet. Add the scallop mixture. Sauté for 3 to 4 minutes or until the scallops are almost cooked. Add the eggs. Cook just until the eggs are firm. Add the sour cream. Cook until no visible raw egg remains, stirring constantly. Serve over toast or grits.

Serves 4

spinach quiche

To ensure that your quiche is creamy and firm instead of watery, remove any excess moisture from the vegetables. Thoroughly sauté or precook the vegetables. To dry them, place the vegetables on a paper towel or a clean cotton towel and gently press out any excess water before filling the crust.

2   (10-ounce) packages frozen chopped spinach
8   ounces (or more) chopped ham
4   eggs, beaten
1   small onion, grated
1 1/2   pounds shredded Monterey Jack cheese
16   ounces cottage cheese, drained
2   unbaked (9-inch) deep-dish pie shells

Cook the spinach using the package directions; drain well. Combine the spinach, ham, eggs and onion in a bowl. Combine the Monterey Jack cheese and cottage cheese in another bowl. Layer 1/4 of the spinach mixture and 1/4 of the cheese mixture in each pie shell. Repeat the layers. Bake at 425 degrees for 15 minutes. Reduce the oven temperature to 350 degrees. Bake for 35 minutes longer or until a knife inserted into the center comes out clean.

Serves 12

Uncommonly Boston — Boston's Central Artery/Tunnel Project, referred to as the "Big Dig," is the largest and most expensive public works project in the country's history.

egg strata

5	cups French bread cubes
2	cups (8 ounces) shredded Cheddar cheese
8	slices bacon, crisp-cooked, crumbled
1/2	cup sliced mushrooms
1	cup chopped tomatoes
1/2	cup asparagus tips
10	eggs, lightly beaten
4	cups milk
1	teaspoon dry mustard
1/2	teaspoon salt
1/4	teaspoon onion powder
>	White pepper to taste

Place the bread cubes in the bottom of a buttered 9×13-inch baking dish. Top with 1/2 of the cheese, the bacon, mushrooms, tomatoes and asparagus. Combine the eggs, milk, dry mustard, salt, onion powder and white pepper in a bowl. Pour over the bread. Top with the remaining cheese. Refrigerate, covered, for 8 to 12 hours.

Remove the strata from the refrigerator 1 hour before baking. Bake at 325 degrees for 1 hour. Let stand before serving.

Serves 12

Uncommonly Boston — Beacon Hill was at the heart of the abolitionist movement in the United States and was the home to more African-American and white abolitionists and underground railroad stations than anywhere else in America.

smoked salmon
and dill frittata

Enjoy this feast for the eyes and taste buds at your next brunch.

When using eggs in a casserole or quiche, remember that room-temperature eggs reach a greater volume when whipped than those taken directly from the refrigerator. To bring eggs to room temperature quickly, place them in a bowl, cover them with tepid water, and let stand for five minutes.

8	eggs
1/4	cup heavy cream
1/2	teaspoon salt
1/4	teaspoon freshly ground pepper
8	ounces smoked salmon fillets, flaked or cut into bite-size pieces
1/4	cup fresh dill weed, finely chopped
1	tablespoon olive oil
1/2	small red onion, diced

Beat the eggs, cream, salt and pepper in a medium bowl until blended. Fold in the salmon and dill; set aside.

Heat the olive oil in an ovenproof nonstick skillet over medium heat. Add the onion. Sauté for 8 minutes or until tender. Add the egg mixture. Cook, without stirring, for 3 to 5 minutes or until the egg is set on the bottom and almost set on the top. Broil 6 inches from the heat source for 1 to 1 1/2 minutes or until the top is golden brown and puffy and no visible raw egg remains. Cool for about 5 minutes. Loosen the frittata from the skillet with a spatula and slide onto a serving plate. Cut into wedges.

Note: If you do not have an ovenproof skillet, cover the skillet handle with foil before placing it under the broiler.

Serves 4 to 6

Photo on page 85

 Uncommonly Boston — Boston is known as the "Cradle of Liberty" because of its instrumental role in the American Revolution.

croque monsieur

With its smoky ham and nutty cheese sauce, this rustic sandwich is a delicious choice for brunch or lunch.

2	tablespoons butter
2	tablespoons flour
1	cup milk
1	large bay leaf
>	Pinch of nutmeg
2	thick slices ham
4	ounces sliced Gruyère cheese or Swiss cheese
4	thick slices white sandwich or country-style bread (such as Tuscan or peasant bread)
1	tablespoon butter, melted
1/4	cup (1 ounce) shredded Gruyère cheese or Swiss cheese

Melt 2 tablespoons butter in a small saucepan over medium heat. Add the flour and stir for 1 minute. Whisk in the milk gradually. Add the bay leaf and nutmeg. Cook over medium-high heat until the sauce is very thick, stirring constantly. Remove and discard the bay leaf. Reduce the heat to low, keeping the sauce warm.

Divide the ham and cheese slices between two of the bread slices. Top with the remaining bread slices, forming two sandwiches. Heat a large heavy skillet over low heat. Brush the outsides of the sandwiches with 1 tablespoon melted butter or spray with nonstick cooking spray. Place the sandwiches in the hot skillet and cook until deep golden brown on both sides.

Remove the sandwiches to a baking sheet. Top evenly with the sauce and shredded cheese. Broil on the top oven rack for 3 to 5 minutes or until the cheese begins to brown.

Serves 2

Uncommonly Boston — Located on Beacon Hill, the Phillips School became the city's first integrated school in the mid-1800s.

cuban pork sandwiches

PAUL O'CONNELL   Chef, Chez Henri Restaurant

Chef O'Connell prepares Cuban fusion dishes that are truly inventive and artfully presented in a casually elegant bistro setting. His menus feature French classics with a Cuban flair and eclectic culinary touches.

PORK

2	cups orange juice
1	cup molasses
1/2	to 3/4 cup chopped garlic
2	tablespoons cumin
3	pounds boneless pork butt
>	Salt and pepper to taste

CHIPOTLE AÏOLI

1/3	cup canned chipotle chiles
1	garlic clove
1/3	cup mayonnaise
2	tablespoons olive oil
>	Salt and pepper to taste

SANDWICHES

8	(6-inch) French bread loaves
1	cup chopped pickles (cornichons or sour dill)
1	pound baked ham, thinly sliced
1 1/2	pounds Gruyère cheese, thinly sliced
1/4	cup (1/2 stick) butter, softened
1/4	cup grainy mustard
>	Plantain chips
>	Salsa

For the pork, combine the orange juice, molasses, garlic and cumin in a small saucepan. Bring to a boil. Remove from the heat. Reserve for a basting sauce. Place the pork butt on a rack in a roasting pan. Season with salt and pepper. Roast at 350 degrees for 1 hour. Reduce the oven temperature to 275 degrees. Baste the pork with some of the reserved sauce. Roast for 5 hours longer or until fork-tender, basting frequently. Let stand until cool. Refrigerate, covered, for 8 to 12 hours to firm up for slicing.

For the chipotle aïoli, combine the chipotle chiles and garlic in a food processor and process until finely chopped. Remove to a bowl. Add the mayonnaise, olive oil, salt and pepper and mix well; set aside.

For the sandwiches, slice the pork butt as thinly as possible. Cut the bread loaves lengthwise into halves. Place cut sides up on a baking sheet. Spread 3 to 4 tablespoons of the chipotle aïoli over the bread halves; top evenly with the pickles. For each sandwich, place two to three ham slices on one bread half and about 4 ounces pork on the other half. Place two cheese slices on each bread half. Bake the sandwiches open face at 350 degrees for 15 to 20 minutes. Remove from the oven and close the sandwiches. Spread the butter and mustard evenly on the outsides of the sandwiches. Cook on a griddle or grill over low to medium heat until golden brown on both sides. Cut the sandwiches into halves. Serve with plantain chips and salsa.

Serves 8

essential chicken salad
with tarragon, grapes and toasted almonds

CHRIS PARSONS   Executive Chef, Catch

Chef Parsons, a fourth generation fly fisherman, focuses on seafood and local produce. His unusual combinations of ingredients are blended perfectly and prepared in a minimalist style, allowing the freshness of the main ingredient to take center stage.

4	boneless skinless chicken breasts, grilled or poached
1	cup seedless red grapes, cut into halves
1/4	cup toasted slivered almonds
2/3	cup extra-virgin olive oil
1/4	cup Champagne vinegar
1	tablespoon Dijon mustard
1	shallot, minced
1/4	cup coarsely chopped fresh tarragon leaves
>	Salt and pepper to taste
1	sourdough baguette, sliced
>	Potato chips

Cut the cooked chicken breasts into 1/2-inch cubes. Combine the chicken, grapes and almonds in a large bowl; set aside.

Whisk the olive oil, vinegar, Dijon mustard, shallot, tarragon, salt and pepper in a bowl. The vinaigrette does not need to be emulsified. Pour over the chicken mixture and toss to coat. Refrigerate, covered, until chilled or for up to 3 days. Serve with the baguette and potato chips.

Serves 4

bellisimo

1	(750-milliliter) bottle Champagne, chilled	1/2	cup peach schnapps
1/2	cup Chambord	1	cup (about) fresh raspberries
		2	peaches, diced (optional)

Combine the Champagne, Chambord and schnapps in a pitcher. Place 3 raspberries and a few peach pieces in the bottom of each Champagne flute. Fill each glass with the Champagne mixture and serve immediately.

Serves 4 to 6

sunday's best bloody marys

8	cups tomato juice	1	tablespoon celery salt
8	cups vegetable juice cocktail	3	cups vodka (optional)
5	ounces Worcestershire sauce	>	Ice
>	Juice of 1/2 lemon	>	Celery stalks for garnish
1	tablespoon salt	>	Olives for garnish
1	tablespoon lemon pepper		

Combine the tomato juice, vegetable juice cocktail, Worcestershire sauce, lemon juice, salt, lemon pepper, celery salt and vodka in a pitcher and mix well. Refrigerate until cold. Serve cold in glasses filled with ice. Garnish with celery stalks and/or olives.

Note: Omit the vodka for Virgin Marys or let guests add their own as desired.

Serves 20

Uncommonly Boston — The first church built by free blacks in America, the African Meeting House, opened on Joy Street in Boston in 1806.

creamy hot chocolate

7	ounces high-quality unsweetened chocolate	>	Pinch of salt
1/2	cup cold water	1	cup heavy whipping cream
3/4	cup sugar	1	teaspoon vanilla extract
		5	quarts milk

Combine the chocolate and cold water in a heavy saucepan. Heat over medium heat until the chocolate is melted and smooth, whisking frequently. Add the sugar and salt. Cook for 3 to 4 minutes, whisking frequently. Remove from the heat; cool. Beat the cream in a mixing bowl until soft peaks form. Add the vanilla. Beat until stiff peaks form. Fold into the chocolate mixture. Heat the milk in a large saucepan until hot. Place a heaping tablespoon of the chocolate base in each cup. Add 1 cup of the hot milk to each cup and stir until smooth.

Serves 20 Photo on page 91

southie irish cream coffee

STAN FRANKENTHALER   Executive Chef and Director Culinary Development, Dunkin' Brands

Chef Frankenthaler and the culinary dream team at Dunkin' Brands use their talent and experience to create new and innovative quick, quality foods. This award-winning team shares a passion for exploration, culinary artistry, and inventiveness. They are dedicated to creating fresh, high-quality, delicious food and flavorful, fun beverages!

14	ounces high-quality dark chocolate, coarsely chopped	5	teaspoons superfine sugar
2	cups heavy cream	8	ounces Irish whiskey (optional)
4	cups strong brewed Dunkin' Donuts coffee	1/4	cup whipped cream
		>	Nutmeg or cinnamon

Place the chocolate in a bowl. Heat 2 cups cream in a saucepan until hot; pour over the chocolate. Cover the bowl until the chocolate melts; stir until smooth. Stir a small amount of the coffee into the chocolate mixture; stir the chocolate mixture into the remaining coffee. Stir in the sugar. Strain the coffee mixture through cheesecloth into a pitcher and chill. Divide the coffee mixture among four tall glasses. Add 2 ounces whiskey to each glass. Top each with 1 tablespoon whipped cream and sprinkle with nutmeg.

Serves 4

Pasta Primavera with Shrimp

PASTAS & grains

The food of the North End is as rich and diverse as the history of its residents. The North End is the birthplace of Paul Revere, who installed the first tower bells in America at the Old North Church. In 1775, Paul Revere took his famous midnight ride when two lanterns were lit and hung in the steeple of the Old North Church to alert Revolutionary troops that the British were arriving by sea. In addition to its famous residences and churches, the North End is also known for the first public playground and the largest money heist in United States history.

Today, 90 percent of the North End's population is of Italian descent, but historically the North End has been home to many different nationalities. During the mid-1600s the North End was segregated from the city of Boston. It was a busy commercial port bordered by water on three sides. Huge mansions and beautiful churches were built, cobblestone streets were laid, and as the tradesmen and shipbuilders moved to the area, the North End quickly became a stylish and desirable neighborhood.

However, by the end of the American Revolution, the area fell out of favor, and nearly a third of the North End's residents moved away. Immigrant populations began to settle in their place. It quickly became overcrowded and afflicted with disease and crime. Nicknamed "Black Sea" and "Murder District," by 1827 the North End was considered a refuge for drunken sailors and scandalous women.

In the mid-1870s, the ethnicity of the population began to change. Slowly, the Italians transformed the neighborhood by turning to what they knew best—their culture. Many opened small family shops featuring the trades they brought with them from Italy. Cobbler shops, butcher shops, bakeries, and restaurants filled the area. In 1919, tragedy struck when a fifty-foot tank exploded and the streets were flooded by 2.3 million gallons of molasses. Twenty-one people died and 150 were injured; more lives were lost than in the Boston Massacre. Despite the devastation, the area was rebuilt and thrived.

Today, Italian food and traditions live on in the North End. A warm summer evening finds families playing cards outside, enjoying weekly neighborhood festivals, or visiting on their front steps. Walking down Hanover Street evokes a feeling of the Old Country; the air is filled with the wonderful smells of sharp cheese, warm bread, and aromatic garlic. There are more than eighty-seven restaurants to choose from, all reflecting the love of food, friends, and family that embodies the spirit of the North End.

Visit the North End for a look into the past and an amazing food experience.

pasta primavera with shrimp

Colorful vegetables and bright pink shrimp make this pasta a feast for the eyes as well as the stomach.

3	cups spiral-shaped pasta	1	tablespoon oregano
2	cups sugar snap peas, trimmed, or green beans	1/4	teaspoon kosher salt
1	tablespoon olive oil	1/4	teaspoon freshly ground pepper
1	pound fresh deveined peeled shrimp	4	cups torn fresh spinach
2	garlic cloves, minced	1 1/2	cups cherry tomatoes, cut into halves
		1	cup crumbled feta cheese

Cook the pasta in a pot of boiling water for 6 minutes, without salt or oil. Add the peas. Cook for 2 minutes; drain. Heat the olive oil in a medium nonstick skillet over medium-high heat. Add the shrimp, garlic, oregano, salt and pepper. Sauté for 3 minutes or until the shrimp turn pink. Combine the pasta mixture, shrimp mixture, spinach, tomatoes and cheese in a bowl and mix well.

Serves 6

Photo on page 92

spinach pesto linguini

12	ounces fresh spinach	6	garlic cloves
1/2	cup fresh basil leaves	1	teaspoon salt
1/2	cup (2 ounces) grated Parmesan cheese	1	pound linguini, cooked, drained
1/2	cup olive oil	1	pint grape tomatoes or cherry tomatoes, cut into halves

Soak the spinach in warm water for 10 minutes, changing the water once. Combine the spinach, basil, cheese, olive oil, garlic and salt in a food processor and process until blended. Toss with the cooked linguini and tomatoes in a bowl.

Serves 4 to 6

linguini with white
clam sauce

Native New England clams are the stars of this simple and flavorful dish.

One pound of spaghetti or linguini yields approximately four servings. One pound of spaghetti should take eight to ten minutes to cook, while linguini should take ten to twelve minutes.

4	(6-ounce) cans good-quality chopped or minced clams	>	Salt and black pepper to taste
1/4	cup (1/2 stick) butter	>	Crushed red pepper to taste
1/4	cup olive oil	1	pound linguini, cooked, drained
2	to 3 garlic cloves, minced		
1/4	cup white wine	>	Freshly grated Parmesan cheese
1	tablespoon oregano		
1	tablespoon parsley	1	lemon, cut into wedges

Drain the clams, reserving the clam juice and clams separately. Heat the butter and olive oil in a large sauté pan over medium heat until the butter melts. Add the garlic. Cook briefly, but do not let it brown. Add the clam juice, wine, oregano, parsley, salt, black pepper and red pepper. Bring to a boil. Reduce the heat to low. Simmer for 15 to 20 minutes, adding the clams during the last few minutes. Cook just until the clams are heated through. Do not overcook or the clams will toughen.

Place the linguini in a bowl and top with the clam sauce. Serve with cheese and lemon wedges.

Serves 4 to 6

Uncommonly Boston — The first sewing machine was invented by Massachusetts farmer Elias Howe in 1844.

pasta bolognese

Try a full-bodied chianti or dry pinot noir with this rich pasta classic.

2	tablespoons olive oil
8	ounces ground beef
8	ounces ground pork
1	small onion, chopped
1	carrot, chopped
3	garlic cloves, minced
1	cup dry white wine
1	(6-ounce) can tomato paste
1/4	cup fresh basil leaves, chopped

1/4	cup fresh mint leaves, chopped
1	teaspoon crushed red pepper
1	(28-ounce) can whole tomatoes
>	Salt and freshly ground black pepper to taste
1/2	cup heavy cream
1	pound spaghetti, fettuccini or ravioli, cooked al dente, drained

Heat the olive oil in a large skillet over medium-high heat. Add the beef and pork. Brown the meats, stirring until crumbly; drain. Add the onion, carrot and garlic. Sauté until the vegetables are tender. Reduce the heat to low. Stir in the wine, tomato paste, basil, mint and red pepper. Cook for 2 to 3 minutes. Add the tomatoes. Bring to a boil. Reduce the heat to low. Simmer for 15 minutes, stirring frequently. Season with salt and black pepper. Stir in the cream. Simmer gently until the sauce is creamy and slightly thickened. Serve over the pasta.

Serves 4 to 6

To prevent pasta from sticking together, be sure to use a large pot with plenty of water and stir when first adding the pasta to the boiling water. Never rinse pasta after cooking. If it isn't going to be used immediately, toss it with a few teaspoons of olive oil and store it in an airtight container.

Uncommonly Boston — St. Leonard's Church, located in the North End, was built in 1873, making it the first Italian church built in New England and the second oldest Italian church in America.

rosemary chicken with rigatoni

DAVE BECKER   Chef/Proprietor, Sweet Basil

Chef Becker creates traditional Italian cuisine that is fresh, well prepared, and delicious. Dave is a man of many talents. In addition to managing the restaurant and cooking, he acted as the food stylist for the Junior League of Boston's cookbook, *Boston Uncommon*.

4	ounces pancetta or bacon, diced		2	plum tomatoes, diced
3	tablespoons olive oil		1/2	cup asparagus pieces, cut 1/2 inch thick
>	Pinch of butter		1/2	cup (2 ounces) grated asiago cheese
3	pounds boneless skinless chicken breasts, cut into 2-inch pieces		1	pound rigatoni, cooked, drained
>	Kosher salt and pepper to taste		3	pinches of chopped fresh parsley for garnish
2	tablespoons (heaping) minced garlic		2	pinches of chopped fresh basil for garnish
2	pinches of chopped fresh rosemary		>	Pinch of grated asiago cheese for garnish
1/2	cup white wine			
2	cups heavy cream			
3/4	cup chicken stock (optional)			

Cook the pancetta in a skillet over low heat until crisp. Reserve the drippings; set aside.

Heat another skillet until hot. Add the olive oil and butter; heat until the butter is browned. Add the chicken; season with salt and pepper. Sear until browned on all sides. Add the pancetta with a small amount of the reserved drippings, the garlic and rosemary. Cook until the garlic is browned. Add the wine and stir to deglaze the pan. Cook until the liquid is almost evaporated. Add the cream, stock, tomatoes, asparagus and 1/2 cup cheese. Cook until the sauce is thickened to the desired consistency, stirring occasionally. Stir in the rigatoni. Garnish with the parsley, basil and cheese.

Serves 6 to 8

shrimp and feta cheese
with rigatoni

2	pounds fresh deveined peeled shrimp	1	cup fresh julienned basil leaves
1/2	cup olive oil	3/4	cup dry white wine
1	to 2 teaspoons crushed red pepper flakes	2	teaspoons oregano
>	Cracked black pepper to taste	1/2	cup tomato sauce
1	pound rigatoni	1/4	cup sambuca or other anise-flavored liqueur
2	teaspoons minced garlic	1/2	cup heavy cream
2	cups roasted red pepper strips	1	cup crumbled feta cheese
		>	Salt and freshly ground black pepper to taste

Noodles with twists or grooves, such as ziti, rigatoni, and cavatappi, tend to hold sauce the best.

Toss the shrimp with 1/4 cup of the olive oil, the red pepper flakes and cracked black pepper in a bowl. Refrigerate, covered, until ready to use. Cook the rigatoni using the package directions; drain.

Heat the remaining 1/4 cup olive oil in a large sauté pan. Add the garlic. Cook for 1 minute; do not brown. Stir in the roasted red peppers. Cook over medium heat for 2 to 3 minutes. Add 1/2 cup of the basil, the wine and oregano. Cook for 5 minutes or until the liquid is reduced. Stir in the tomato sauce and sambuca. Cook for 5 minutes longer.

Push the sauce mixture to the edge of the pan. Increase the heat to medium-high. Add the shrimp mixture to the center of the pan. Cook for 3 to 4 minutes or until the shrimp turn pink. Combine the shrimp with the sauce mixture in the pan and mix well. Stir in the cream and cheese. Cook for 3 to 4 minutes or until the cheese melts slightly and the sauce comes together, stirring frequently. Add the rigatoni and toss to coat. Top with the remaining 1/2 cup basil. Season with salt and ground black pepper. Serve immediately.

Serves 6

Uncommonly Boston — The celebration of Christmas was banned in Boston from 1659 to 1681 because the Puritans believed it was a decadent practice.

soba noodle salad
with vegetables and tofu

Fresh and dried pasta require different cooking times. Fresh pasta cooks very quickly; therefore, as soon as the pasta rises to the surface of the water, begin checking for doneness. Dried pasta should be cooked using the directions on the package and checked one or two minutes before the end of the stated cooking time.

DRESSING

1/2	cup low-sodium soy sauce
1/4	cup packed brown sugar
2	tablespoons orange juice
1	tablespoon sesame seeds, toasted
1	tablespoon minced gingerroot
1	tablespoon rice vinegar
2	teaspoons dark sesame oil
1	teaspoon minced garlic
1	teaspoon chile paste with garlic

SALAD

8	ounces soba noodles, cooked, drained (about 4 cups)
3	cups very thinly sliced napa cabbage
1	(12-ounce) package firm tofu, drained, cut into 1-inch cubes
1	cup shredded carrots
1/2	cup fresh cilantro leaves
2	cups fresh bean sprouts

For the dressing, whisk the soy sauce, brown sugar, orange juice, sesame seeds, gingerroot, vinegar, oil, garlic and chile paste in a bowl.

For the salad, combine the noodles, cabbage, tofu, carrots and cilantro in a large bowl. Drizzle with the dressing and toss well to coat. The salad may be covered and refrigerated at this point. Add the bean sprouts just before serving.

Serves 4 Photo on page 101

Uncommonly Boston — In 1950 the Boston Celtics made history by drafting Charles ("Chuck") Cooper, the first African-American player in professional basketball.

peanut-chili noodles
with chicken and shrimp

To peel and devein shrimp, remove the head and, starting at the large end, use your fingers to pry open and pull back the first few sections of shell. Grasp the end of the tail between your fingers and gently tug to remove the rest of the shell. Once the shell has been removed, make a shallow cut along the dark vein on the shrimp's back. Gently lift out the vein using the tip of a sharp knife. Once they have been peeled and deveined, rinse the shrimp in cool water and refrigerate.

MARINADE

1/4 cup sesame oil
> Juice of 2 limes
2 tablespoons rice wine vinegar
2 tablespoons soy sauce
2 tablespoons chili oil
2 garlic cloves, minced
2 teaspoons honey
12 fresh peeled deveined shrimp
3 boneless skinless chicken breasts, cut into strips

DRESSING

3 tablespoons peanut butter
3 tablespoons soy sauce
3 tablespoons sesame oil
> Juice of 1 lime

2 tablespoons ground ginger
2 teaspoons sugar
> Hot red pepper flakes to taste

ASSEMBLY

2 garlic cloves, minced
2 tablespoons chili oil
1 red bell pepper, sliced
5 (3-ounce) packages ramen noodles, seasoning packets discarded
2 (8-ounce) cans water chestnuts, drained and sliced
8 ounces snow peas, sliced, blanched
3 green onions, chopped

For the marinade, combine the sesame oil, lime juice, vinegar, soy sauce, chili oil, garlic and honey in a bowl. Place the shrimp and chicken in separate sealable plastic bags. Pour 1/2 of the marinade over each; seal the bags. Marinate in the refrigerator for at least 2 hours.

For the dressing, combine the peanut butter, soy sauce, sesame oil, lime juice, ginger, sugar and red pepper flakes in a bowl; set aside.

To assemble, remove the chicken and shrimp from the marinade; discard the marinade. Sauté the chicken and garlic in the chili oil in a skillet. Add the bell pepper and shrimp. Cook until the shrimp turn pink and the chicken is cooked through. Remove from the heat; set aside. Cook the noodles in boiling water using the package directions; drain. Place in a large bowl. Pour the dressing over the noodles. Add the chicken mixture, water chestnuts, snow peas and green onions and toss.

Serves 4 to 6

greek pasta salad

8	ounces mostaccioli or other tubular pasta	1/2	cup olive oil
8	ounces feta cheese, crumbled	2	tablespoons cider vinegar
3	Roma tomatoes, diced	2	tablespoons lemon juice
1	cup chopped black olives	1	teaspoon oregano
1	onion, chopped	1	garlic clove, minced
		1/2	teaspoon salt

Cook the mostaccioli using the package directions; drain. Combine the mostaccioli, cheese, tomatoes, olives and onion in a large bowl. Whisk the olive oil, vinegar, lemon juice, oregano, garlic and salt in a small bowl. Pour over the salad and toss gently. Refrigerate, covered, until chilled. Toss gently before serving.

Serves 4 to 6

sausage and pasta
with mushrooms

An earthy barolo or a peppery babaresco nicely complements the savory flavors of sausage and herbs in this pasta dish.

12	ounces tube-shaped pasta	3/4	cup chopped onion
3	tablespoons extra-virgin olive oil	5	garlic cloves, minced
1	pound cooked chicken sausage or turkey sausage, thickly sliced	10	ounces fresh baby spinach
12	to 16 ounces mushrooms, thickly sliced	1 1/4	cups chicken broth
		>	Freshly grated Romano or Parmesan cheese

Cook the pasta using the package directions; drain and set aside.

Heat the olive oil in a large pan over medium-high heat. Add the sausage, mushrooms, onion and garlic. Sauté for 8 to 10 minutes or until the mushrooms begin to brown. Add the spinach and broth. Cook for 2 to 3 minutes or until the spinach wilts, stirring frequently. Add the pasta and toss. Serve with cheese.

Serves 4

penne saint-tropez

1	pound penne	1	(15-ounce) can crushed tomatoes
>	Salt to taste	>	Pepper to taste
1	large onion, finely minced	1/2	cup heavy cream
5	tablespoons olive oil	1/2	cup (2 ounces) shredded Swiss cheese
3	tablespoons butter		

Cook the penne in boiling salted water using the package directions; drain. Cook the onion in the olive oil and butter in a heavy covered saucepan over low heat for 20 minutes or until lightly browned, stirring occasionally to prevent the onion from burning. Add the tomatoes, salt and pepper. Cook, covered, over medium-low heat for 20 to 30 minutes. Stir in the cream and adjust the seasonings. Add the pasta and cheese and toss. Serve immediately.

Serves 4 to 6

pasta with prosciutto

1	large onion, chopped	1 1/2	(14-ounce) cans crushed tomatoes (about 2 2/3 cups)
4	garlic cloves, diced	>	Chopped fresh parsley to taste
3	tablespoons olive oil	1	pound pasta, cooked al dente
12	ounces diced imported prosciutto	>	Grated Romano cheese

Sauté the onion and garlic in the olive oil in a large skillet. Add the prosciutto. Cook until the prosciutto changes color. Add the tomatoes and parsley. Bring to a boil. Reduce the heat to low. Simmer, covered, for 1 hour. Toss the pasta with the sauce. Serve with cheese.

Serves 6

Uncommonly Boston — Massachusetts is not referred to as a state. It is known as a Commonwealth: a body of people that form themselves into a free, sovereign, and independent body politic.

lobster risotto milanese

Classic Italian with a distinctly New England flair—rich and creamy risotto pairs well with succulent lobster.

2	chicken lobsters, fully cooked		1	pound arborio rice
10	cups seafood stock or chicken stock		1/2	cup dry white wine
1/2	teaspoon saffron threads		1/2	cup (2 ounces) grated Parmesan cheese
3	tablespoons butter		2	tablespoons fresh parsley, finely chopped
1	onion, chopped		>	Salt and pepper to taste

Shell the lobsters and cut the meat into bite-size pieces. Refrigerate, covered, until ready to use.

Heat the stock in a saucepan over medium-low heat until hot. Crumble the saffron into 1 cup of the hot stock. Let stand for 10 minutes; set aside.

Melt the butter in a large saucepan over medium heat. Reduce the heat to low. Add the onion. Sauté until translucent; do not brown. Increase the heat to medium. Stir in the rice. Cook for 5 minutes, stirring frequently. Add the wine. Cook until absorbed, stirring constantly. Add the saffron mixture. Simmer until the liquid is absorbed, stirring frequently. Add the remaining stock 1 cup at a time, simmering after each addition until the stock is completely absorbed and stirring constantly. When the rice is creamy and tender, fold in the lobster meat and cheese. Cook for 2 minutes or until heated through. Remove from the heat. Stir in the parsley, salt and pepper. Serve immediately.

Serves 6

Transform a simple pasta or risotto dish into a gourmet appetizer or meal by adding shellfish, prosciutto, mushrooms, fresh vegetables, herbs, or cheese.

Uncommonly Boston — Boston-area native John Hancock was the first official signer of the Declaration of Independence.

risotto with mushrooms

Smooth and creamy, this dish is accented by the earthy flavor of porcini mushrooms.

2 1/2	cups chicken broth	1/3	cup freshly grated Romano cheese
1	ounce dried porcini mushrooms	1	tablespoon butter or margarine
2	cups lukewarm water	>	Kosher salt and freshly ground pepper to taste
2	tablespoons extra-virgin olive oil	1	cup button mushrooms, sliced, lightly sautéed in 1 tablespoon butter
1	tablespoon butter or margarine	>	Snipped fresh chives for garnish
2	tablespoons finely chopped onion	1/2	cup (2 ounces) freshly grated Romano cheese
1	cup arborio rice		
1/4	cup white wine		

Bring the broth to a simmer in a saucepan over low heat. Soak the porcini mushrooms in the lukewarm water in a bowl for 30 minutes. Remove mushrooms from the bowl by hand and squeeze out as much water as possible. Strain the soaking liquid through cheesecloth or a coffee filter to remove any residue; reserve the liquid. Rinse the mushrooms in several changes of fresh water; pat dry with paper towels. Coarsely chop the mushrooms; set aside.

Heat the olive oil and 1 tablespoon butter in a heavy pan over medium-high heat. Add the onion. Cook until translucent, stirring constantly. Add the rice. Cook for about 2 minutes or until opaque, stirring constantly. Stir in the wine. Cook for 1 minute or until the liquid is evaporated. Add the hot broth 1/2 cup at a time, simmering after each addition until the broth is completely absorbed and stirring frequently. When the rice has cooked for 10 minutes, add the porcini mushrooms and 1/2 of the reserved soaking liquid. Cook until the liquid is evaporated, stirring constantly. Repeat with the remaining soaking liquid. Continue to cook the rice for about 20 minutes, adding the broth as needed, until the rice is tender but firm to the bite. Remove from the heat. Add 1/3 cup cheese and 1 tablespoon butter; stir until the cheese melts and clings to the rice. Season with salt and pepper. Top with the button mushrooms. Garnish with chives. Serve immediately with 1/2 cup cheese.

Serves 4 to 6

Photo on page 106

When a recipe calls for dried mushrooms to be rehydrated, consider breaking the mushrooms into small pieces before placing them in the liquid. The smaller pieces hydrate more quickly and because the mushrooms have already been broken into bite-size pieces, there's no need to chop them before incorporating them into the recipe.

cashew pineapple rice

2   *tablespoons butter*

1   *tablespoon canola oil*

1   *yellow onion, finely chopped*

1 1/2   *cups long grain rice (do not use instant or quick-cooking)*

1   *(20-ounce) can pineapple chunks*

3   *cups reduced-sodium vegetable broth*

2   *carrots, chopped*

1/2   *cup raw unsalted cashews, lightly toasted*

1/2   *teaspoon salt*

1/2   *teaspoon red pepper flakes*

Heat the butter and canola oil in a medium saucepan. Add the onion. Cook for 4 minutes or until tender. Pour the onion and drippings into a 9×11-inch baking dish. Add the rice, stirring to coat. Drain the pineapple, reserving 1 tablespoon of the juice. Add the pineapple, reserved juice, broth, carrots, cashews, salt and pepper flakes to the rice mixture and stir to combine. Bake, covered, at 350 degrees for 45 to 55 minutes or until the liquid is absorbed. Let stand, covered, for 5 minutes.

Serves 10

Uncommonly Boston — Appointed in 1933, Boston native Frances Perkins was the first female member of a U.S. presidential cabinet.

middle eastern rice pilaf

Ground lamb with the fragrance of cinnamon and cardamom makes this an exotic and satisfying dish.

1/2	cup (1 stick) butter	1 1/2	teaspoons salt
1	(3-ounce) package sliced almonds	1 1/2	teaspoons cinnamon
3	ounces pine nuts	3 1/4	cups water
1	pound ground lamb	1/2	teaspoon cardamom
1	tablespoon ground allspice	1	cup uncooked rice

Melt the butter in a large skillet. Add the almonds and pine nuts. Cook gently until golden brown, stirring frequently and watching carefully to prevent burning. Remove from the skillet; set aside.

Brown the ground lamb with the allspice, salt and cinnamon in the same skillet, stirring until the lamb is crumbly; drain. Add the water, cardamom and almond mixture. Bring to a boil. Stir in the rice. Return to a boil. Cover and reduce the heat to low. Simmer for 15 to 20 minutes or until the rice is tender and all of the liquid has been absorbed.

Serves 4

tabouli

1	(6-ounce) package Parmesan couscous	1	(15-ounce) can black olives, finely chopped, or 1 cup chopped kalamata olives
1	tablespoon fresh parsley, finely chopped		
2	large tomatoes, diced	1	large bunch cilantro, chopped
1	(14-ounce) can black beans, rinsed, drained	>	Juice of 1 lime
		1	tablespoon extra-virgin olive oil
1/2	large red onion, finely chopped	>	Salt and pepper to taste

Cook the couscous using the package directions, adding the parsley during the stand time. Cool; set aside.

Combine the tomatoes, beans, onion, olives, cilantro, lime juice, olive oil, salt and pepper in a bowl. Stir in the cooled couscous. Serve at room temperature for the best flavor.

Serves 4 to 6

Sesame-Shallot Asparagus

VEGETABLES
& sides

South Boston's proximity to Boston Harbor and the Harbor Islands makes it a truly unique neighborhood. South Boston has been known as a predominantly Irish community since the nineteenth century. Between 1845 and 1850, Ireland was devastated by the potato famine. During that period, over 100,000 Irish immigrated to Boston. The immigrants first landed on Deer Island, one of Boston's Harbor Islands, often disease stricken and poor. The Irish immigrants persevered. By the late 1800s, the Irish outnumbered all other ethnic groups in Boston. After decades of struggle, the Irish seized political power in Boston. At the turn of the twentieth century, Boston was known for its largely Irish-American political leadership, and South Boston was known as a tightly knit neighborhood, alive with Irish tradition.

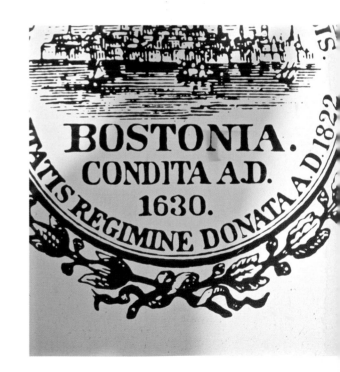

South Boston, known to locals as "Southie," borders the city of Boston and the Boston Harbor. Triple-decker houses, a hallmark of South Boston, were built to accommodate multi-generational families and the needs of this densely populated neighborhood. Today, South Boston still looks and feels like a tightly knit community. Residents typically patronize local shops and meet friends for a pint at their favorite local tavern. Many of the restaurants and pubs have an Irish flair.

South Boston never seems more Irish than on Saint Patrick's Day. Every year on March 17, the entire community celebrates the holiday with fervor, culminating in the Saint Patrick's Day Parade. Neighbors throw all-day parties, and Irish pubs are alive with laughter and song late into the night.

South Boston is uniquely situated at the gateway to Boston Harbor. The streets of the neighborhood slope down to the shore. Parks, walkways, benches, playgrounds, and picnic tables line the waterfront and attract residents and visitors alike. Local piers and docks bustle with boating and fishing activity. The shores of South Boston provide a view to some of the Boston Harbor Islands, a national park made up of thirty-four islands. From South Boston, a wide promenade leads to Castle Island, a historic fortress and park. Fort Independence, first established in 1634 and now a park, is located on Castle Island. It saw battle during the American Revolution, protected the harbor during the War of 1812, and was used by the Navy during Word War II.

Explore South Boston's Irish heritage and charming harbor-side location.

sesame-shallot asparagus

1 pound fresh asparagus, ends trimmed
2 tablespoons peanut oil or sesame oil
2 shallots, minced
1 tablespoon soy sauce
1 tablespoon sesame seeds
2 tablespoons lemon juice

Steam the asparagus in a vegetable steamer for 3 to 4 minutes or just until tender. Do not overcook. Plunge the asparagus into cold water to stop the cooking; set aside.

Heat the peanut oil in a large skillet. Add the shallots. Cook until tender. Add the asparagus. Cook for 1 to 2 minutes on each side, drizzling with the soy sauce and sprinkling with the sesame seeds.

Arrange the asparagus on a serving dish. Drizzle with the lemon juice. Serve immediately.

Serves 4

Photo on page 110

When preparing asparagus, remove the tough ends by holding the end of the stalk in one hand and the tip in the other. Bend the spear until it breaks naturally. The asparagus typically breaks at the point where the stalk becomes tough.

guess-again carrots

2 pounds carrots, thinly sliced or shredded
8 ounces sharp Cheddar cheese, shredded
1 onion, grated
2 tablespoons butter
1/2 teaspoon salt
1/8 teaspoon pepper
1/2 to 1 cup bread crumbs
> Butter for topping (optional)

Cook the carrots in boiling water in a saucepan until tender; drain and mash. Stir in the cheese, onion, 2 tablespoons butter, the salt and pepper. Spoon into a buttered 1-quart baking dish. Sprinkle with the bread crumbs; dot with butter. Bake at 350 degrees for 40 minutes.

Serves 8

carrot, parsnip and pea au gratin

1/4	teaspoon onion powder	12	ounces frozen pearl onions, thawed
5	large carrots, cut into 1-inch pieces	1	cup heavy cream
5	large parsnips, cut into 1-inch pieces	>	Salt and freshly ground pepper to taste
12	ounces frozen peas, thawed		

Generously butter a 2-quart baking dish. Sprinkle the onion powder over the bottom.

Combine the carrots, parsnips, peas and onions in a medium bowl. Add the cream; season with salt and pepper. Stir until all the vegetables are coated with cream. Pour into the prepared baking dish, scraping the bowl to remove all of the cream.

Bake at 375 degrees for 45 to 75 minutes or until the casserole is bubbly and golden brown on top and the vegetables are tender, stirring halfway through the cooking time. Serve immediately.

Serves 6

corn casserole

This casserole is great served as a side dish with baked ham or roasted meat.

1	(15-ounce) can cream-style corn	1	cup chopped onion, sautéed (optional)
1	(8-ounce) can whole kernel corn, drained	1	cup chopped green bell pepper or red bell pepper (optional)
1	(8-ounce) package corn muffin mix	1	cup sour cream
1	cup (4 ounces) shredded Cheddar cheese	1/2	cup (1 stick) butter, melted
		2	eggs, beaten

Combine the cream-style corn, whole kernel corn, muffin mix, cheese, onion, bell pepper, sour cream, butter and eggs in a bowl and mix well. Pour into a greased 9×13-inch baking pan. Bake at 350 degrees for 35 minutes.

Serves 8

cumin and cilantro
corn skillet

1   red bell pepper, chopped
1   tablespoon butter
1 1/2   teaspoons cumin

1   (16-ounce) package frozen corn, thawed
1/3   cup fresh cilantro leaves, minced

Sauté the bell pepper in the butter in a large nonstick skillet until tender. Stir in the cumin. Cook for 30 seconds. Add the corn and cilantro. Sauté for 2 minutes or until heated through.

Serves 4   Photo on page 143

leeks au gratin

8   large leeks
2   tablespoons butter
12   ounces plain Havarti cheese, cut into 1/4×3-inch strips

5   large potatoes, peeled, thinly sliced
5   slices bacon, crisp-cooked, crumbled
1/2   cup (about) heavy cream

Trim and discard the roots and tough greens from the leeks. Leaving the leeks intact, wash them thoroughly to remove embedded sand. Cook the whole leeks in boiling water until fork-tender. Place the leeks side-by-side in a shallow baking dish, slicing each lengthwise down the center to create a long pocket. Immediately spread the butter along the interior of each leek; top with the cheese, breaking the strips to fit if necessary. Arrange the potato slices between the leeks. Sprinkle with the bacon. Pour enough cream over the top to almost cover the potatoes; do not cover the cheese.

Bake at 350 degrees for 45 minutes or until the potatoes are tender. Broil for a few minutes until the cheese is melted and browned.

Serves 4

Preserve the delicate flavor of sweet summer corn by freezing it for up to six months. Boil shucked fresh corn for two minutes and then quickly cool the ears by placing them in an ice water bath or under running water. Cut the corn kernels from the cobs using a sharp knife and then freeze the kernels in a sealable plastic freezer bag.

onion casserole

 5 to 6 slices white bread, such as Pepperidge Farm
 1 tablespoon butter
12 onions, thinly sliced
 8 ounces American cheese, shredded
 1 egg
 1 cup milk
 1 teaspoon salt
1/2 teaspoon pepper
 1 teaspoon celery seeds

Toast the bread slices. Butter the toast and remove the crusts. Cut into small pieces. Place the onion slices in a large saucepan. Add enough water to cover. Bring to a boil. Boil until tender; drain. Layer the toast pieces, onions and cheese 1/2 at a time in a buttered 2-quart baking dish.

Beat the egg lightly in a small bowl. Add the milk, salt, pepper and celery seeds and mix well. Pour over the layers. Bake at 375 degrees for 40 minutes or until hot and bubbly.

Serves 8 to 10

Uncommonly Boston — The Boston Light, site of the first lighthouse in North America, is the last remaining manned light station in the United States.

refrigerator mashed potatoes

A make-ahead dish, these potatoes are perfect for a dinner party or buffet.

5 pounds potatoes, cut into cubes	1 teaspoon onion salt
6 ounces cream cheese, softened	1/2 teaspoon (or more) pepper
1 cup sour cream	2 tablespoons butter
1 teaspoon salt or garlic salt	

Cook the potatoes in boiling water in a saucepan until tender; drain and mash. Combine the potatoes and cream cheese in a mixing bowl with a mixer. Add the sour cream, salt, onion salt and pepper. Beat until fluffy. Refrigerate, covered, until ready to heat. (May be prepared up to several days in advance.)

Spoon the mashed potatoes into a greased baking dish. Dot with the butter. Bake at 350 degrees for 30 minutes or until heated through.

Serves 10   *Photo on page 181*

roasted rosemary red potatoes

The flavors of rosemary and nutmeg make these potatoes something special.

2 tablespoons olive oil	1 tablespoon minced garlic
2 pounds small red potatoes, cut into quarters	1 tablespoon rosemary, crushed
	1/8 teaspoon nutmeg
1 tablespoon finely chopped green onions	> Salt and pepper to taste

Heat the olive oil in a large nonstick skillet over medium-high heat. Add the potatoes, green onions, garlic, rosemary and nutmeg; toss well. Cook and stir for 2 to 3 minutes or until the potatoes are hot. Remove to a baking sheet sprayed with nonstick cooking spray. Season with salt and pepper. Bake at 400 degrees for 30 to 60 minutes or until the potatoes are golden brown and almost tender; baking time is determined by the size of the potatoes.

Serves 6

boston baked beans

A cabernet sauvignon or côtes du rhône would provide a beautiful contrast to the smoky and sweet flavor of traditional baked beans.

The pilgrims learned how to make baked beans from the Native Americans. Beans were placed in earthenware pots and cooked in pits covered with hot rocks. Puritan custom forbade women from cooking on Sunday; therefore, beans and traditional brown bread that were to be eaten on both Saturday and Sunday were cooked on Saturday night and kept warm until the next morning.

3	cups dried small white beans
12	ounces salt pork
1	large onion, peeled
6	tablespoons molasses
1/2	teaspoon salt
1/2	teaspoon prepared mustard
1/2	teaspoon pepper
>	Boiling water

Sort and rinse the beans. Place in a large saucepan and add enough water to cover. Soak for 8 to 12 hours. Drain the beans; return to the saucepan and cover with fresh water. Cook over medium heat until a thick layer appears on the surface of the water. Remove from the heat; drain.

Score the rind on the salt pork at 1/2-inch intervals. Place the salt pork and onion in the bottom of a bean pot. Spoon the beans over the pork. Top with the molasses, salt, prepared mustard and pepper. Pour enough boiling water over the beans to cover.

Bake, covered, at 250 degrees for 4 hours, adding more boiling water to cover the beans every hour if necessary. Uncover the beans; move the salt pork to the top. Bake, uncovered, for 1 hour longer or until the salt pork is crisp. Do not add any water during the final baking time.

Serves 10 to 12

Photo on page 119

 Uncommonly Boston — The navy bean is the official vegetable of Massachusetts and the original bean of Boston Baked Beans.

baked squash casserole

3	pounds butternut squash, peeled, cut into chunks
1/2	cup chopped onion
2	eggs, lightly beaten
1/4	cup (1/2 stick) butter
1	tablespoon sugar
1	teaspoon salt
1/2	teaspoon pepper
>	Dash of cinnamon (optional)
>	Dash of nutmeg (optional)
1/4	cup (1/2 stick) butter, melted
1/2	cup bread crumbs

Cook the squash in boiling water in a saucepan until tender; drain and mash. Combine the squash, onion, eggs, 1/4 cup butter, the sugar, salt, pepper, cinnamon and nutmeg in a bowl and mix well. Spoon into a greased 7×11-inch baking dish. Pour the melted butter over the squash mixture. Sprinkle the bread crumbs over the top. Bake at 375 degrees for 1 hour.

Serves 6 to 8

Uncommonly Boston — The Declaration of Independence was first read from the balcony of the Old State House, Boston's oldest surviving public building.

squash with cranberry
and orange

The full, rich flavors of a pinot noir or beaujolais would nicely balance the tanginess of the cranberry and orange in this delectable dish.

4   small acorn squash,
    cut into halves, seeded

>   Salt to taste

1   cup fresh cranberries,
    chopped

1   large orange, peeled, diced

2   tablespoons butter, melted

2   tablespoons dark
    brown sugar

Sprinkle the squash cavities with salt. Place the squash halves cut side down in a baking dish. Bake at 350 degrees for 25 minutes.

Combine the cranberries, orange and butter in a bowl. Spoon into the squash cavities. Bake for 25 minutes longer or until the squash is tender. Sprinkle the brown sugar evenly over the fruit filling. Broil until bubbly.

Serves 8

Winter squash have a high water content and should feel heavy for their size. Those that don't feel heavy may be drying out and developing a stringy texture. Winter squash maintain the best flavor when they are cold-weather harvested and stored in cool temperatures to develop their sugars.

Uncommonly Boston — The first known apple orchard in New England was planted in 1629 by the Massachusetts Bay Colony.

bourbon sweet potatoes

3   (23-ounce) cans sweet
    potatoes, drained, or
    3 pounds sweet potatoes,
    cooked, mashed
1   cup sugar
1   cup milk
4   eggs, beaten

1/2 cup (1 stick) butter, melted
1/2 cup bourbon
1   teaspoon salt
1   teaspoon vanilla extract
1/2 teaspoon cinnamon
1/2 to 1 cup miniature
     marshmallows (optional)

Combine the sweet potatoes, sugar, milk, eggs, butter, bourbon, salt, vanilla and cinnamon in a large bowl and mix well. Pour into a greased large soufflé dish or 9×13-inch baking dish.

Bake at 350 degrees for 45 to 60 minutes or until a knife inserted into the center comes out clean. Top evenly with the marshmallows. Bake for 10 to 15 minutes longer.

Serves 8 to 12   Photo on page 168

Uncommonly Boston — Boston is known as "Beantown" because molasses, a key ingredient in baked beans, was plentiful in Boston during the heyday of the rum and sugar trade.

zucchini-stuffed tomatoes

Beautiful to look at and delicious to eat, these tomatoes are a great side dish.

3	large zucchini, shredded (2¹/₂ pounds)	>	Chopped fresh rosemary leaves to taste
1	teaspoon salt	>	Chopped fresh basil leaves to taste
2	tablespoons butter		
1	tablespoon olive oil	>	Grated Parmesan cheese to taste
3	tablespoons minced scallions	5	large tomatoes
3/4	cup heavy cream	>	Salt to taste
>	Chopped fresh thyme leaves to taste		

Place the zucchini in a colander; sprinkle with 1 teaspoon salt. Let drain for 15 to 20 minutes. Place in a clean kitchen towel and squeeze to remove all excess liquid; set aside.

Melt the butter with the olive oil in a sauté pan over medium heat. Add the scallions. Cook for 1 minute. Increase the heat to medium-high. Add the zucchini. Cook for about 5 minutes or until tender, tossing frequently. Stir in the cream. Cook until the mixture is thickened and the cream is absorbed. Add thyme, rosemary, basil and cheese.

Cut the tomatoes crosswise into halves. Scoop out and discard the seeds and flesh. Sprinkle the tomato halves with salt to taste; place on a baking sheet. Fill with the zucchini mixture. Bake at 425 degrees for 10 minutes or until tender, but not mushy.

Serves 10

For the best flavor, select young zucchini that are slender and measure four to six inches long. They should have thin skin, tiny seeds, and sweet flesh that is tender but firm. Large zucchini may taste bitter and have a mealy texture.

baked cherry tomatoes

3/4	cup fresh bread crumbs		3/4	teaspoon thyme
1/4	cup fresh parsley leaves, chopped		>	Salt and pepper to taste
2	tablespoons freshly grated Parmesan cheese		4	cups cherry tomatoes or grape tomatoes, cut into halves
1	shallot, minced		>	Olive oil
1	garlic clove, minced			

Combine the bread crumbs, parsley, cheese, shallot, garlic, thyme, salt and pepper in a bowl and mix well. Place the tomatoes in a baking dish. Top with the bread crumb mixture. Drizzle with olive oil. Bake at 450 degrees for 10 to 15 minutes.

Serves 8 to 10   Photo on page 125

creamy herbed spinach

1	tablespoon olive oil or butter		6	ounces boursin cheese, crumbled
1	onion, chopped		1/2	cup (2 ounces) shredded Parmesan cheese
2	(10-ounce) packages frozen spinach, thawed, drained		>	Parmesan cheese for topping (optional)

Heat a skillet over medium-high heat. Add the olive oil and heat until hot. Add the onion. Sauté for 5 minutes or until tender. Stir in the spinach and mix well. Remove from the heat. Add the boursin cheese and 1/2 cup Parmesan cheese and mix well. Top with additional Parmesan cheese.

Serves 4 to 6

When cooked, the volume of fresh spinach reduces considerably. One pound of fresh spinach will cook down to approximately one cup. When making a side dish with cooked spinach, plan on using eight ounces of fresh spinach per person.

far east vegetables and tofu

1	tablespoon vegetable oil	3/4	cup canned unsweetened coconut milk
2	large garlic cloves, minced	2	tablespoons brown sugar
1	teaspoon minced gingerroot	2	tablespoons soy sauce
1	red bell pepper, cut into thin strips	1	tablespoon sesame oil
1	small Chinese or Japanese eggplant, cut into 1-inch pieces	1/2	teaspoon cayenne pepper, or to taste
8	small broccoli florets	1	(2-inch) square baked teriyaki-seasoned tofu, cut into 1/4×1/2×1-inch pieces
8	small cauliflower florets		
6	large shiitake mushrooms, stems removed, caps sliced	1	green onion, cut into 1-inch pieces
		1/3	cup peanuts, toasted, chopped
8	snow peas, strings removed	4	cups hot cooked brown rice

Heat the vegetable oil in a large nonstick skillet over medium-high heat. Add the garlic and gingerroot. Cook for 30 seconds, stirring constantly. Add the bell pepper, eggplant, broccoli, cauliflower, mushrooms and snow peas. Cook, covered, for 6 minutes or until the vegetables are almost tender, stirring occasionally.

Combine the coconut milk, brown sugar, soy sauce, sesame oil and cayenne pepper in a small bowl until well blended. Add to the vegetables. Cook for 2 minutes. Stir in the tofu and green onion. Cook, covered, for about 2 minutes or just until the vegetables are tender and coated with sauce. Sprinkle with the peanuts. Serve over the rice.

Note: May substitute regular eggplant, cut into small cubes, for the Chinese or Japanese eggplant.

Serves 4

Uncommonly Boston — In 1877, Helen Magill White became the first woman to earn a Ph.D. in the United States; the degree was conferred by Boston University.

harvest soft tacos

These tacos are filled with a great combination of fall vegetables and flavorful seasonings.

2	cups cubed butternut squash or acorn squash
8	ounces fresh baby spinach
1	tablespoon water
1	tablespoon vegetable oil
1	small onion, diced
1	jalapeño chile, finely chopped
2	garlic cloves, minced

1	(15-ounce) can black beans, drained
1	teaspoon oregano
1/2	teaspoon cumin
3	to 4 tablespoons cider vinegar, or to taste
>	Salt and pepper to taste
1	to 2 ounces goat cheese, crumbled
6	corn tortillas

Steam the squash in a large pot over 1/2 inch water for about 15 minutes or until tender; drain and set aside. Steam the spinach over 1 tablespoon water for about 2 minutes or until wilted; set aside.

Heat the oil in a medium skillet over medium heat. Add the onion, jalapeño chile and garlic. Sauté for about 8 minutes or until the onion is translucent. Stir in the beans, oregano and cumin. Season with the vinegar, salt and pepper. Add the squash and spinach. Fold in the cheese gently.

Wrap the tortillas in damp paper towels. Microwave on High for 20 to 30 seconds or until warm. Fill the tortillas with the bean mixture.

Serves 4 to 6

 Uncommonly Boston — Massachusetts was the birthplace of four American presidents: John Adams, John Quincy Adams, John Fitzgerald Kennedy, and George Herbert Walker Bush.

red lentil dal

The aromatic spices and hearty lentils in this dish make it a flavorful side dish or a perfect vegetarian entrée.

1	cup red lentils
2	tablespoons olive oil
1	red or yellow onion, chopped
2	ribs celery, chopped
2	carrots, chopped
2	garlic cloves, minced
1	tablespoon grated gingerroot, or 1 teaspoon ground ginger
1/2	teaspoon cumin
1/2	teaspoon (or more) curry powder
2	cups water
1	(14-ounce) can vegetable broth or chicken broth
>	Salt and pepper to taste
>	Hot cooked brown rice or basmati rice (optional)
>	Fresh cilantro sprigs for garnish
>	Lemon slices for garnish

Sort and rinse the lentils; set aside.

Heat the olive oil in a large saucepan. Add the onion, celery, carrots and garlic. Cook until tender. Stir in the gingerroot, cumin and curry powder. Cook for 1 minute. Add the water, broth and lentils and mix well. Bring to a boil. Reduce the heat to low. Simmer, covered, for 20 to 30 minutes or until the lentils are tender. To thicken the dal, simmer a little longer. To thin it, add more water. Season with salt and pepper.

Serve in bowls as is or over rice. Garnish with cilantro sprigs and lemon slices.

Serves 4 to 6

roasted vegetable tzimmes

6   sweet potatoes, cut into 1-inch cubes

8   fresh prune plums, cut into halves, pitted

1   large onion, cut into eighths

5   carrots, thickly sliced

1/4   cup extra-virgin olive oil

>   Salt and black pepper to taste

1/2   teaspoon cinnamon

1/4   teaspoon salt

1/4   teaspoon freshly ground black pepper

1/4   teaspoon cayenne pepper

1/4   cup honey

2   tablespoons cider vinegar

2   tablespoons orange juice

1   tablespoon grated orange zest

1/4   cup (1/2 stick) unsalted butter, melted, cooled slightly

Place the sweet potatoes, plums, onion and carrots in a large roasting pan. Drizzle with the olive oil and season with salt and black pepper to taste; toss to combine. Roast at 400 degrees for 1 hour or until the vegetables are very tender, stirring halfway through the roasting time.

Combine the cinnamon, 1/4 teaspoon salt, 1/4 teaspoon black pepper and the cayenne pepper in a small bowl. Add the honey, vinegar, orange juice and orange zest and blend well. Whisk in the butter in a fine stream and continue whisking until well blended. Pour over the roasted vegetables and toss gently. Season with salt and black pepper to taste.

Note: May substitute purple plums, cut into quarters, for the prune plums.

Serves 8

Uncommonly Boston — The first Children's Museum in the area was opened in Jamaica Plain in 1913.

Boiled Lobster, York Harbor Style

SEAFOOD & shellfish

Charlestown, Faneuil Hall, and the Quincy Market echo the history of Boston's seaport. Settled in 1628, Charlestown was named for King Charles I. The town was located on a peninsula, which Native Americans called Mishawam. Charlestown, which joined the City of Boston in 1847, is a tightly knit neighborhood, rooted in history and its seaside tradition. Charlestown featured prominently in the history of the Revolutionary War. The historic Battle of Bunker Hill took place in Charlestown on June 17, 1775. On the fiftieth anniversary of the battle, the Bunker Hill Monument was erected to commemorate this turning point in the war. The monument, a 221-foot granite obelisk, is a distinctive landmark. Charlestown's thirteen wharves were a hub for a thriving fishing industry and nineteenth-century importing and exporting. A Charlestown citizen, Fredric Tudor, the "Ice King," revolutionized shipping by introducing the use of pond-cut ice blocks for packaging. This allowed the local Baldwin apple to be shipped worldwide with guaranteed freshness.

The Charlestown Navy Yard is home to the oldest Marine barracks and the USS *Constitution*. Known as Old Ironsides, the USS *Constitution* is the world's oldest commissioned warship. The *Constitution* is one of the sixteen historic sites on Boston's Freedom Trail. Travelers in search of history can follow the red brick path of the Freedom Trail from Charlestown to Faneuil Hall and through Quincy Market.

Faneuil Hall and Quincy Market stand side by side. Built in 1742, historic Faneuil Hall became the designated meeting place for Bostonians to discuss civic affairs. Samuel Adams spoke here to support a call to arms against the British in pre-Revolutionary America. Faneuil Hall was lost to fire in 1761 but was soon reconstructed and nicknamed the "Cradle of Liberty," as a symbol of Boston's freedom. The lower level of Quincy Market was once used as docks. By the early 1800s, Quincy Market was essentially Boston's first organized shopping center. New England farmers and fishermen came to Quincy Market to sell produce, meats, and fish. Today, Faneuil Hall and Quincy Market are a center of commerce and entertainment. They house more than 125 different shops and eateries featuring American, Asian, Mexican, Indian, and Italian cuisine, among others. One block away is Haymarket, the largest farmer's market in Boston. Local restaurant owners go to Haymarket for the best selection of fresh fruits and vegetables. The Boston Harbor and the Fish Piers are nearby with fresh seafood delivered to their docks daily. Near Quincy Market is the Union Oyster House, the oldest restaurant in America, renowned for its seafood and raw bar.

Visit Charlestown, Faneuil Hall, and Quincy Market to experience Boston's historical waterfront and to enjoy the freshest seafood and local neighborhood dining.

boiled lobster
york harbor style

Put on your bib and take out the lobster crackers. Nothing says
New England like a boiled lobster feast!

1	(12-ounce) bottle beer, at room temperature (preferably Samuel Adams or Red Stripe)	1/2	cup (1 stick) butter	
2	(1 1/4- to 1 1/2-pound) lobsters	1	to 2 garlic cloves, minced	
		1/2	cup white wine	

Fill a large lobster pot with enough water to cover the lobsters. Bring
the water to just below a boil. Add the beer. Bring the liquid to a full
boil. Add the lobsters. Boil, covered, for 10 to 12 minutes or until the
lobsters are uniformly red. Remove from the pot.

Melt 1/4 cup of the butter in a small saucepan. Add the garlic. Cook
until lightly browned. Add the remaining 1/4 cup butter and the wine.
Heat until the butter melts, stirring constantly. Divide the butter
sauce between two small bowls. Serve with the lobster.

Serves 2   Photo on page 130

Uncommonly Boston — New England clam chowder has been served
at every U.S. presidential inauguration since 1981.

Prepare the ultimate lobster dinner.

Select a large pot that will hold enough

water to cover the lobsters completely.

Bring the water to a boil and add

1 tablespoon salt per quart of water.

Place the lobsters in the pot, claws first.

When the water returns to a boil, begin

timing. The cooking time depends on

the size of the lobster. One-pound

lobsters take five minutes; two pounds or

more take twelve minutes. Remove the

lobsters from the pot. Use kitchen shears

to snip the lobster claws, holding the

lobster over the sink to let the water

drain from the claws. Serve on a white

platter and garnish with lemon wedges

and greens.

easy steamed clams

24	cherrystone clams in shells, well scrubbed	2	plum tomatoes, sliced
1	tablespoon salt	2	shallots, sliced
1	tablespoon cornmeal	2	tablespoons parsley flakes, or 1/4 cup fresh parsley leaves, chopped
1/2	cup water		
1/2	cup dry white wine	2	garlic cloves, minced
1/4	cup (1/2 stick) butter	8	ounces vermicelli, cooked, drained

Place the clams in a large bowl. Add enough cold water to cover. Sprinkle the salt and cornmeal over the water. Let stand at room temperature for 1 hour.

Combine 1/2 cup water, the wine, butter, tomatoes, shallots, parsley and garlic in a large microwave-safe dish. Microwave, covered, on High for 5 minutes; stir.

Remove the clams from the water and rinse. Place in a single layer in the wine mixture. Microwave, covered, on High for 5 minutes or until the clams open, stirring halfway through the cooking time. Discard any clams that do not open. Serve the clams and sauce over the vermicelli.

Serves 2

Uncommonly Boston — America's oldest seaport is located in Massachusetts. Established in 1623, Gloucester is the heart of New England's fishing industry.

crab crepes with melba sauce

CRAB FILLING

16 ounces cream cheese, softened

12 ounces thawed frozen crab meat or canned crab meat, rinsed, drained

8 ounces sour cream

1 tablespoon dried onion flakes, or 1/4 cup minced onion

1/2 teaspoon salt

1/4 teaspoon garlic powder

1/4 cup (1/2 stick) butter

1 cup chopped pecans

SAUCE

2 cups raspberries

1/2 cup confectioners' sugar

1/4 cup apple juice

1 tablespoon fresh lemon juice

ASSEMBLY

20 prepared crepes, warmed

> Chopped pecans for garnish

For the crab filling, combine the cream cheese, crab meat, sour cream, onion flakes, salt and garlic powder in a bowl and mix well. Spread evenly in a deep 9-inch round baking dish. Bake at 350 degrees for 30 minutes.

Melt the butter in a skillet. Add the pecans. Cook until browned. Spoon the pecans over the crab mixture. Bake for 20 minutes longer. Cool for 5 minutes.

For the sauce, combine the raspberries, confectioners' sugar, apple juice and lemon juice in a blender and process until smooth. Pour the sauce through a fine mesh strainer; discard the solids.

To assemble, spoon the crab mixture into the warm crepes; fold each crepe in half to enclose the filling. Drizzle the melba sauce over the crepes. Garnish with pecans. Serve warm.

Serves 10 to 12

Uncommonly Boston — The Charlestown Navy Yard is home to the USS *Constitution*, also known as "Old Ironsides," the oldest commissioned warship in the world.

beacon hill baked scallops

1	pound fresh scallops	2	tablespoons butter
1	shallot, minced	2	tablespoons flour
2	cups (about) dry white wine	1/4	teaspoon salt
4	to 6 tablespoons butter	1/4	teaspoon pepper
1	(1/4-inch-thick) slice Canadian bacon, chopped	1/2	cup light cream
2	green onions, minced	1/2	cup (2 ounces) shredded Cheddar cheese
20	small fresh mushrooms, sliced	>	Paprika for garnish
1/4	cup chopped green bell pepper	>	Fresh parsley for garnish
1	garlic clove, minced		

Cut the scallops into halves or quarters if they are large. Place the scallops and shallot in a 2-quart saucepan with enough wine to cover. Bring to a boil. Reduce the heat. Simmer for 5 minutes. Remove the scallops with a slotted spoon and arrange in four small buttered ramekins or a buttered 9×9-inch baking dish. Simmer the shallots and wine until the wine is reduced by 1/2.

Heat 4 to 6 tablespoons butter in a skillet until melted. Add the bacon, green onions, mushrooms and bell pepper. Sauté until tender. Add the garlic and stir to combine. Spoon into the reduced wine mixture and set aside.

Heat 2 tablespoons butter in a saucepan over low heat. Whisk in the flour. Add the wine mixture, salt and pepper and blend until the sauce is medium-thick and smooth. Remove from the heat. Add the cream and mix well. Pour over the scallops. Sprinkle the cheese over the top. Bake in a preheated 400-degree oven for 15 minutes or until hot and bubbly and the cheese has melted. Garnish with paprika and parsley.

Serves 4

Uncommonly Boston — Richard Fairbanks' tavern in Boston was established as the first post office in the United States in 1639.

lemon-parsley broiled scallops

1	pound sea scallops	2	teaspoons minced parsley
2	tablespoons fresh lemon juice	1	teaspoon grated lemon zest
1	tablespoon water	2	garlic cloves, minced
1	tablespoon olive oil	1/2	teaspoon freshly ground pepper

Place the scallops in a shallow 2 1/2-quart baking dish. Combine the lemon juice, water, olive oil, parsley, lemon zest, garlic and pepper in a bowl and mix well. Pour over the scallops. Marinate, covered, in the refrigerator for 10 to 15 minutes.

Uncover the scallops. Broil 5 1/2 inches from the heat source for about 6 minutes; stir well. Broil for 6 minutes longer or until the scallops are tender.

Serves 4

greek shrimp with feta cheese

2	teaspoons olive oil	12	ounces large fresh deveined peeled shrimp
1 1/2	cups chopped tomatoes		
1/2	cup chopped onion	1/2	cup crumbled feta cheese
2	garlic cloves, crushed	1	teaspoon oregano
		>	Salt and freshly ground pepper to taste

Heat the olive oil in a medium nonstick skillet over medium-high heat. Add the tomatoes, onion and garlic. Sauté for 3 minutes. Add the shrimp. Top with the cheese and oregano. Sauté for 3 minutes or until the shrimp turn pink. Remove from the heat. Let stand, covered, for 2 minutes or until the cheese melts. Season with salt and pepper.

Serves 2

gloucester shrimp
and scallops

There are three kinds of scallops—bay scallops, sea scallops, and calico scallops. New England harvests both bay and sea scallops. Bay scallops are smaller, and many claim they are sweeter than sea scallops.

2	tablespoons butter	1/3	cup finely chopped shallots
1	pound sea scallops	1/4	teaspoon tarragon
8	ounces large fresh deveined peeled shrimp	1/2	cup heavy cream
1/2	cup white wine vinegar	1	tablespoon Dijon mustard
1/2	cup chicken broth	>	Salt and white pepper to taste

Melt the butter in a skillet over medium-high heat. Add the scallops and shrimp. Cook just until the scallops are tender and the shrimp turn pink. Remove the shellfish to a bowl, reserving the drippings in the skillet.

Add the vinegar, broth, shallots and tarragon to the drippings. Bring to a boil. Cook until the liquid is reduced to 1/2 cup. Stir in the cream, Dijon mustard and any accumulated juices from the bowl of shellfish. Return to a boil. Cook until the liquid is reduced to 3/4 cup. Stir in the shellfish. Season with salt and white pepper.

Serves 4

Uncommonly Boston — The first toothpick was used in the United States at the Union Oyster House near Faneuil Hall in Boston.

cod and littlenecks
in almond-tomato sauce

RICHARD VELLANTE Executive Chef and Senior Vice-President, Legal Sea Foods

Chef Vellante is dedicated to serving absolutely the freshest fish and finest seafood meals. His innovative and creative menus highlight the highest quality ingredients, providing guests with memorable and delicious dining experiences.

1/2	cup olive oil	1/2	cup fresh basil leaves, julienned
1	tablespoon chopped garlic	1	teaspoon sugar
>	Pinch of hot red pepper flakes	1	teaspoon fresh thyme, chopped
1	cup sliced Spanish onion	>	Salt and black pepper to taste
1	(14-ounce) can whole tomatoes	1 1/2	pounds codfish fillets
1/2	cup almonds, chopped	>	Olive oil for brushing
1/2	cup drained capers	12	fresh littleneck clams in shells

Heat 1/2 cup olive oil in a saucepan over medium heat. Add the garlic and red pepper. Cook for 2 minutes or until lightly browned. Add the onion. Cook over low heat for 10 to 12 minutes or until softened, stirring occasionally. Crush the tomatoes into the pan with your hands, adding all the juices. Stir in the almonds, capers, basil, sugar, thyme, salt and black pepper. Bring to a simmer. Cook for 10 minutes. Remove from the heat. (May be prepared one day ahead. Refrigerate, covered, until ready to use.)

Spoon the almond-tomato sauce in the center of a baking dish. Lightly brush the codfish with olive oil; season with salt and black pepper. Place over the sauce. Arrange the clams around the fish and sauce. Bake at 350 degrees for 15 to 20 minutes or until the fish flakes easily and the clams open. Discard any clams that do not open.

Serves 4

pan-seared haddock with
sweet corn, chanterelle mushrooms,
tiny green beans and corn sorrel nage

CHRISTOPH LEU   Executive Chef, Turner Fisheries, Westin Copley Place

Chef Leu handpicks the freshest local seafood and finest ingredients, then transforms them into culinary masterpieces. His New England–inspired menus are both traditional and creative and evoke the feeling of the sea.

1 ear of corn, husked	3 ounces dry vermouth or dry white wine
8 ounces tiny green beans	3/4 cup lobster stock or vegetable stock
> Salt to taste	1 teaspoon German winter thyme or garden thyme
2 pounds haddock fillets	
> Sea salt and freshly ground white pepper to taste	> Juice of 1 lemon
	4 ounces chanterelle mushrooms
3 tablespoons butter	4 sorrel leaves, chopped
1 tablespoon chopped shallots	

Simmer the corn in salted water in a saucepan for 4 minutes. Cut the kernels from the cob; set aside. Blanch the beans in boiling salted water in a saucepan for 3 minutes. Plunge the beans into ice water to stop the cooking; set aside.

Cut the haddock into eight 4-ounce portions. Season with sea salt and white pepper. Melt 1 1/2 tablespoons of the butter in a skillet over medium-high heat. Place the haddock skin side down in the skillet. Sear until the fish is golden brown on both sides and flakes easily. Remove from the skillet; keep warm.

Add the shallot and 1/2 of the corn to the skillet. Sauté for 1 minute. Add the vermouth and stir to deglaze the pan. Cook until the liquid is reduced to 2 tablespoons. Add the stock and thyme. Cook until the sauce is reduced to 1/2 cup. Purée the sauce in a blender. Season with the lemon juice, sea salt and white pepper; keep warm.

Sauté the mushrooms in the remaining 1 1/2 tablespoons butter in the skillet for 2 minutes. Add the remaining corn and beans. Season with the sorrel, salt and white pepper.

Arrange the vegetable mixture in the center of a serving plate. Place the haddock skin side up on top. Drizzle with the sauce.

Serves 4

herb-coated flounder fillets

A contemporary take on the Friday night New England fish supper.

1 1/2 cups panko (Japanese bread crumbs)	1 pound flounder fillets, skinned
1/2 to 3/4 cup minced fresh parsley leaves	1/4 cup Dijon mustard
1/2 cup minced scallions	1 1/2 tablespoons butter
1 egg, beaten	1 1/2 tablespoons olive oil
1 teaspoon water	

Combine the bread crumbs, parsley and scallions in a large bowl; toss to mix. Combine the egg and water in a shallow dish. Brush the flounder generously with the Dijon mustard. Dip into the egg mixture and then into the bread crumb mixture to coat. Press the coating into the fillets.

Heat the butter and olive oil in a skillet over medium heat. Add the flounder. Cook for about 3 minutes per side or until the fish is golden brown and flakes easily.

Serves 4

broiled halibut

This is seafood at its simplest and most delicious.

2 pounds halibut fillets or other white fish fillets	1/4 cup butter, melted
2 tablespoons lemon juice	3 tablespoons minced onion
1/2 cup (2 ounces) grated Parmesan cheese	3 tablespoons mayonnaise
	1/4 teaspoon salt

Brush the halibut with the lemon juice. Broil for 6 to 8 minutes. Combine the cheese, butter, onion, mayonnaise and salt in a bowl. Spread over the halibut. Broil for 2 to 3 minutes longer or until the topping is bubbly and the fish flakes easily.

Serves 4 to 6

pacific halibut with littleneck clams
vidalia onions, green garlic, peas and salsa verde

TOM FOSNOT   Executive Chef, blu at The Sports Club/LA

Chef Fosnot's menu features seasonal American dishes inspired by fresh flavors and classic European techniques. His dishes are simple and elegant with a contemporary flair that complements the ambience of this sleek eatery.

FISH FUMET

5	pounds fish bones, roasted
1	gallon water
2	cups white wine
6	ribs celery, sliced
3	onions, sliced
2	leeks, sliced and trimmed
1	fennel bulb, greens removed, sliced
8	parsley stems
6	thyme stems
4	bay leaves
8	peppercorns

SALSA VERDE

2	cups fresh parsley leaves
1/4	cup fresh tarragon leaves
3	garlic cloves, sliced
1	tablespoon drained capers
1	tablespoon chopped cornichons
1 1/2	cups extra-virgin olive oil

For the fish fumet, combine the fish bones, water, wine, celery, onions, leeks, fennel, parsley, thyme, bay leaves and peppercorns in a stockpot. Bring to a boil. Reduce the heat to low. Simmer for 30 minutes; strain and set aside.

For the salsa verde, combine the parsley, tarragon, garlic, capers, cornichons and olive oil in a food processor and process until well mixed; set aside.

HALIBUT AND ASSEMBLY

1/4	cup vegetable oil	12	fresh littleneck clams in shells
4	to 5 ounces halibut steaks	2	cups fish fumet or fish stock
>	Salt and pepper to taste	1/2	cup white wine
2	ounces chorizo, diced	1	cup peas
1	Vidalia onion, thinly sliced	1/4	cup chopped fresh parsley
2	stalks green garlic, sliced, or 3 garlic cloves, sliced	2	tablespoons butter
		1/4	cup salsa verde

For the halibut, heat the vegetable oil in a large sauté pan. Season the halibut with salt and pepper. Add to the pan. Sear until golden brown on both sides. Remove from the pan; set aside. Drain any drippings from the pan.

Cook the chorizo in the same pan for 1 minute to render the fat. Add the onion and green garlic. Sauté for 1 minute. Add the clams, fish fumet and wine. Cook until the clams begin to open. Return the halibut to the pan. Cook until the fish flakes easily. Discard any clams that do not open. Remove the halibut to a serving bowl. Place the clams around the halibut.

Return the liquid in the pan to a boil. Add the peas, parsley and butter. Cook until heated through. Adjust the seasonings; pour over the halibut. Spoon 1/4 cup of the salsa verde over the halibut.

Serves 4

Uncommonly Boston — The first full cargo of bananas to reach the U.S. arrived at Boston's Long Wharf in 1871.

pecan-crusted salmon

This versatile dish makes a fast weeknight supper or beautiful dinner party entrée.

1/2	cup pecans, chopped	4	teaspoons honey
1/2	cup fresh parsley leaves, chopped	2	teaspoons Dijon mustard
1/2	cup bread crumbs	4	(6-ounce) salmon fillets
2	tablespoons butter, melted		

Combine the pecans, parsley and bread crumbs in a bowl; set aside. Combine the butter, honey and Dijon mustard in another bowl. Place the salmon on a foil-lined baking sheet. Spread the butter mixture over the salmon. Top with the bread crumb mixture, patting to coat. Bake at 450 degrees for 10 to 15 minutes or until the fish flakes easily.

Serves 4

Photo on page 144

char-grilled salmon steaks

6	(12-ounce) salmon steaks	>	Salt and pepper to taste
6	tablespoons olive oil	2	tablespoons butter, softened
1	tablespoon paprika (preferably Hungarian)	2	teaspoons chopped fresh parsley leaves

Brush the salmon steaks on both sides with the olive oil. Season with the paprika, salt and pepper. Place the salmon on an oiled grill over hot coals or in an oiled grill pan heated in a 375-degree oven. Grill or bake at 375 degrees for 3 minutes. To make diamond-shaped grill marks, rotate the salmon at a 45-degree angle. Cook for 2 minutes longer. Turn the salmon over and repeat. Grill or bake until the fish flakes easily. Remove to a serving plate.

Combine the butter and parsley in a bowl. Brush over the salmon.

Serves 6

baked salmon
with cucumber herbed cream sauce

Marinades or rubs add great flavor to fish. Marinate seafood in the refrigerator. Discard used marinade as it contains raw fish juices.

MARINADE

1/2	cup dry white wine
1/2	cup orange juice
1/4	cup soy sauce
1	orange, sliced
2	tablespoons fresh dill weed
1/2	shallot, finely chopped
4	(6- to 8-ounce) salmon fillets with skin

SAUCE

1	cup packed fresh baby spinach, stems removed
1	cup packed escarole, torn into pieces
1/2	shallot
1	cup light sour cream
1/4	cup fresh dill weed sprigs, or to taste
1/4	cup chopped fresh parsley leaves
3	tablespoons coarse-grain Dijon mustard
2	tablespoons fresh lemon juice
1	cup chopped seeded peeled cucumber
1/8	teaspoon salt
1/8	teaspoon pepper

For the marinade, combine the wine, orange juice, soy sauce, orange slices, dill weed and shallot in a shallow dish. Place the salmon flesh side down in the marinade. Refrigerate, covered, for 2 to 3 hours, turning the fillets every 30 minutes.

For the sauce, combine the spinach, escarole and shallot in a food processor and process until finely chopped. Add the sour cream, dill weed, parsley, Dijon mustard and lemon juice and process until smooth. Remove to a medium bowl. Fold in the cucumber, salt and pepper; set aside.

Remove the salmon from the marinade; discard the marinade. Place the salmon skin side down on a foil-lined baking sheet. Bake at 450 degrees for 14 to 16 minutes or until the fish flakes easily. Remove to warm plates. Top with the sauce.

Serves 4

roast salmon with
fresh corn, tomatoes and zucchini

The flavors of summer marry the fresh flavors of the sea in this tasty dish.

2	tablespoons fresh lemon juice
1	tablespoon grated lemon zest
2	garlic cloves, minced
1	tablespoon fresh lemon thyme leaves, minced
1	teaspoon fresh rosemary leaves, minced
>	Kosher salt and freshly ground pepper to taste
3	tablespoons extra-virgin olive oil
4	(6-ounce) salmon fillets, skinned
2	tablespoons butter
1	cup fresh corn kernels (about 4 to 5 ears)
2	zucchini, sliced
2	yellow squash or crookneck squash, sliced
1	small red bell pepper, thinly sliced
20	red and/or yellow cherry tomatoes
2	tablespoons chopped fresh chives
>	Lemon wedges for garnish

Fish is best cooked quickly with high heat. Gauge the cooking time by measuring the fish at its thickest part. For every inch of thickness, cook for eight to ten minutes. Determine if the fish is done by noting its color and the flakiness of the flesh. Slip the point of a sharp knife into the flesh and pull aside; the edges should be opaque and the center slightly translucent with flakes just beginning to separate.

Combine the lemon juice, lemon zest, garlic, 2 teaspoons of the lemon thyme, the rosemary, salt and pepper in a small bowl. Whisk in the olive oil gradually and continue whisking until the mixture emulsifies. Place the salmon in a shallow dish. Pour the marinade over the salmon. Refrigerate, covered, for at least 2 hours, turning the fillets several times.

Melt the butter in a large cast-iron skillet over medium-high heat until foamy. Add the corn, zucchini, squash, bell pepper and remaining 1 teaspoon lemon thyme. Season with salt and pepper. Sauté for about 4 minutes or until the vegetables are lightly browned.

Remove the salmon from the marinade; discard the marinade. Place the salmon over the vegetables in the skillet. Add the tomatoes. Roast at 400 degrees for 10 to 15 minutes or until the fish flakes easily. Top with the chives. Garnish with lemon wedges.

Note: May substitute roasted red peppers for the red bell pepper for a richer flavor.

Serves 4

parker house schrod

GERRY TICE   Executive Chef, Parker's Restaurant, Parker House Hotel

Chef Tice celebrates New England cuisine with a contemporary flair. His greatest talent is giving nostalgic cuisine an upscale twist.

1	cup milk
1/2	cup olive oil
2	teaspoons paprika
2	teaspoons Worcestershire sauce
1	teaspoon lemon juice
>	Salt and pepper to taste
6	(8-ounce) haddock or baby cod fillets
4	ounces butter crackers, finely crushed
1	cup (2 sticks) butter, melted
1/2	cup white wine

Combine the milk, olive oil, paprika, Worcestershire sauce, lemon juice, salt and pepper in a shallow dish. Place the cod in the marinade. Refrigerate, covered, for at least 2 hours (the longer the better).

Remove the cod from the marinade; discard the marinade. Dip the fillets in the cracker crumbs to coat well. Place in a buttered baking pan. Drizzle with the butter. Pour the wine around the cod, not over it. Bake at 400 degrees for about 10 minutes or until the fish flakes easily. Do not overcook. Broil for a few minutes to add some color.

Serves 6

Uncommonly Boston — The first American railroad was built in Quincy in 1826 to transport the granite used to build the Bunker Hill Monument in Charlestown.

herb-roasted sea bass
with salsa verde

SALSA VERDE

1	cup extra-virgin olive oil
1	cup fresh Italian parsley leaves, chopped
1/3	cup chopped fresh chives
1/3	cup fresh lemon juice
1/4	cup drained capers, chopped
2	to 3 garlic cloves, minced
2	teaspoons fresh thyme leaves, chopped
2	teaspoons fresh oregano leaves, chopped
1	teaspoon fresh rosemary leaves, chopped
>	Salt and pepper to taste

FISH

6	(8-ounce) sea bass fillets
1/4	cup extra-virgin olive oil
3	tablespoons fresh lemon juice
>	Salt and pepper to taste
3	tablespoons fresh thyme leaves, chopped
3	tablespoons fresh oregano leaves, chopped
2	tablespoons fresh Italian parsley leaves, chopped

For the salsa verde, combine the olive oil, parsley, chives, lemon juice, capers, garlic, thyme, oregano and rosemary in a medium bowl. Season with salt and pepper; set aside.

For the fish, place the sea bass on an oiled baking sheet. Brush with the olive oil and drizzle with the lemon juice. Season with salt and pepper. Combine the thyme, oregano and parsley in a bowl. Sprinkle over the fillets.

Bake at 450 degrees for about 10 minutes or until the fish flakes easily. Serve on warm plates topped with the salsa verde.

Serves 6

Scrod is an acronym for "special catch received on dock." When spelled without an "h," it is young cod or pollock. When spelled with an "h," schrod is haddock. Scrod is often found on Boston restaurant menus but rarely seen outside of New England. No matter how it is spelled, it is a white fish that is lean and firm.

Uncommonly Boston — Natives and longtime residents of Charlestown refer to themselves as "townies."

japanese grilled
marinated swordfish

Hearty swordfish steaks are infused with delicate Asian flavors.

1	cup tamari	2	tablespoons minced garlic
1/2	cup sesame oil	2	teaspoons minced gingerroot
1/2	cup lime juice		
1/4	cup sweet sake	4	(1-inch-thick) swordfish steaks
3	tablespoons red pepper flakes	>	Vegetable oil

Combine the tamari, sesame oil, lime juice, sake, red pepper, garlic and gingerroot in a shallow dish. Add the swordfish to the marinade. Marinate for 10 minutes. Remove the swordfish from the marinade; discard the marinade. Dip the swordfish into vegetable oil. Grill for 5 to 7 minutes on each side or until the fish flakes easily.

Serves 4

swordfish with
avocado-mango salsa

2	(1-inch-thick) swordfish steaks (about 1 pound)	1	large ripe tomato, chopped
1	tablespoon olive oil	1	avocado, chopped
1	teaspoon salt	1/2	yellow bell pepper, chopped
1	teaspoon pepper	1/2	ripe mango, chopped
1/2	bunch scallions, white and green parts, chopped	2	tablespoons chopped fresh cilantro leaves
		>	Salt and pepper to taste

Brush both sides of the swordfish with the olive oil. Sprinkle with 1 teaspoon salt and 1 teaspoon pepper. Place on a broiler pan. Broil for 4 to 5 minutes per side or until the fish flakes easily. Combine the scallions, tomato, avocado, bell pepper, mango and cilantro in a bowl. Season with salt and pepper to taste. Serve over the swordfish.

Serves 2

fusion tuna

A full, spicy red wine, such as an Australian shiraz, zinfandel, or primitivo, pairs nicely with this meaty fish dish.

SALSA

1	large mango, finely chopped
1/2	cup canned black beans
1/2	red bell pepper, chopped
1/4	red onion, chopped
1/4	cup red pepper-seasoned rice vinegar
2	tablespoons sesame oil
>	Juice of 1/2 lime
1/4	jalapeño chile, chopped
>	Cumin to taste

FISH

4	(6-ounce) tuna steaks
>	Salt and pepper to taste
>	Cumin to taste
>	Juice of 1/2 lime
1	avocado, sliced
>	Fresh cilantro for garnish

Tuna and salmon steaks are best served rare in the center. For best results, cook them quickly over very high heat to sear the outside of the steak, leaving the inside pink.

For the salsa, combine the mango, beans, bell pepper and onion in a bowl. Whisk the vinegar, sesame oil, lime juice, jalapeño chile and cumin in another bowl. Pour over the mango mixture and toss to coat; set aside.

For the fish, rub the tuna steaks with salt, pepper and cumin. Drizzle with the lime juice. Grill or broil the tuna to the desired doneness. Serve with the salsa and avocado. Garnish with cilantro.

Serves 4

Uncommonly Boston — Ninety percent of all American lobsters are caught in New England waters.

Turkey Burgers with Apple and Brie

POULTRY & fowl

The diversity of the community and its distinctive squares give Cambridge a unique feel. Cambridge, Massachusetts, was named by its founding fathers after Cambridge, England. It was founded in 1630 by Puritans looking to build a more biblically centered community. By the American Revolution, Cambridge was an established farming village anchored by a large common and Harvard College. Through the years, Cambridge has been recognized as the home to those seeking religious freedom, abolitionists, and liberals. The city is known for its diverse ethnic, philosophical, and intellectual community. The Charles River separates Cambridge from the city of Boston. The Longfellow Bridge is known to locals as the Salt & Pepper Bridge because of the two distinctive granite towers atop the central piers. The bridge spans the Charles River and connects the two cities. First built in 1793, the Longfellow Bridge was named after notable Cambridge citizen and poet Henry Wadsworth Longfellow in 1927.

Cambridge is known as the city of squares. The squares of Cambridge are located where major streets intersect, and they serve as neighborhood centers. Kendall Square is located where the Longfellow Bridge meets the edge of the campus of the Massachusetts Institute of Technology (MIT). Kendall Square is the home of a thriving scientific community and the center of Cambridge's biotech industry. Neighboring the MIT campus are several industrial plants; among them is the Kendall Boiler & Tank Company from which the square gets its name.

Harvard Square is located by Harvard University, the oldest university in the United States. Harvard Square is near the center of Cambridge and is known for its eclectic feel and diverse population, from the Harvard professors to the rebellious street punks. At one time, Harvard Square held the record for having more bookstores per square block than any other place in America.

Located north of Central Square, Cambridge's "downtown" area, and just around the corner from Harvard Square, lies Inman Square. Inman Square is home to the oldest women's-run bookstore in the United States, delis, bakeries, and coffee houses for Cambridge's huge student population. Porter Square is located along the border between Cambridge and the city of Somerville. It was named after an area landmark, the Porter House Hotel. The hotel is no longer in existence, but the hotel's specialty, a porterhouse steak, keeps the legacy of the hotel alive.

Cambridge welcomes students and new residents from all over the world. The diversity of the community is reflected in the variety of international restaurants, the prevalence of ethnic specialty markets, and the abundance of cultural celebrations. For an eclectic dining and cultural experience, visit the squares of Cambridge.

turkey burgers
with apple and brie

1 pound ground turkey

1/2 onion, diced

1/4 cup dark beer

1 teaspoon Worcestershire sauce

> Salt and pepper to taste

3 tablespoons olive oil

1 (12-inch) loaf Italian bread, cut crosswise into quarters

2 Granny Smith apples, cut into 1/4-inch slices

2 ounces Brie cheese, cut into 4 slices

1 cup arugula

Combine the turkey, onion, beer, Worcestershire sauce, salt and pepper in a bowl. Divide into quarters; shape into four patties. Brush both sides of the patties with 1 tablespoon of the olive oil. Split each bread quarter lengthwise. Brush the cut sides of the bread and both sides of the apple slices with the remaining 2 tablespoons olive oil.

Grill the apple slices to desired doneness; set aside. Grill the turkey patties until cooked through, turning once. Top each with a cheese slice and heat until melted. Grill the bread cut sides down until toasted.

Serve the burgers on the grilled bread topped with the apple slices and arugula.

Serves 4

Photo on page 152

For a healthier burger, make your patties using ground turkey or ground turkey breast. Ground turkey is a blend of white and dark meat, or all dark meat, and is generally 85 percent lean. Ground turkey breast is all white meat and is typically up to 99 percent fat free.

Uncommonly Boston — Harvard College, the first American university, was founded in Cambridge in 1636.

turkey meat loaf

To prevent meat loaf from sticking, place one or two slices of bacon on the bottom of the pan. The bacon helps to ease the meat loaf from the pan and adds great flavor.

3 large zucchini, coarsely shredded
2 pounds ground turkey
3/4 cup bread crumbs
1/3 cup ketchup
1 egg
1 tablespoon spicy mustard
1 envelope onion soup mix
1/2 teaspoon garlic powder
1/2 teaspoon thyme

Press the zucchini between paper towels to remove all excess moisture. Combine the zucchini, ground turkey, bread crumbs, ketchup, egg, mustard, soup mix, garlic and thyme in a bowl and mix well. Shape into a loaf. Place in a 9×13-inch baking dish (do not place in a loaf pan).

Bake at 350 degrees for about 1 1/2 hours or until the turkey is cooked through and a meat thermometer registers 175 degrees.

Serves 4 to 6

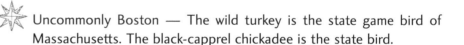 Uncommonly Boston — The wild turkey is the state game bird of Massachusetts. The black-capprel chickadee is the state bird.

chicken salad on the charles

Fresh herbs and vegetables make this a tasty alternative to traditional chicken salad.

1 1/2	pounds boneless skinless chicken breasts (about 4)		5	tablespoons chopped fresh mint leaves
1	cup low-sodium chicken broth		5	tablespoons chopped fresh cilantro leaves
4	scallions, white and green parts, chopped		1/4	cup fresh lime juice
1/4	teaspoon salt		1/4	cup soy sauce
1 1/4	pounds green cabbage, shredded (about 1/2 head)		4	teaspoons sugar
4	carrots, shredded		1/4	cup dry-roasted peanuts, chopped
1	cup peas or snow peas		1/2	cup shredded unsweetened coconut (optional)

Cut each chicken breast into about 5 strips. Combine the broth, 1/4 of the scallions and the salt in a medium saucepan. Bring to a simmer. Stir in the chicken. Cook, covered, over low heat for about 5 minutes. Remove from the heat. Let stand, covered, for 5 minutes or until the chicken is cooked through. Remove the chicken from the pan; cool. Shred into bite-size pieces.

Combine the chicken, remaining scallions, cabbage, carrots, peas, 4 tablespoons of the mint and 4 tablespoons of the cilantro in a large serving bowl. Whisk the lime juice, soy sauce and sugar in a small bowl. Pour over the salad and toss. Add the peanuts and coconut. Sprinkle with the remaining 1 tablespoon mint and 1 tablespoon cilantro.

Serves 4

Uncommonly Boston — The Head of the Charles, one of the world's largest crew regattas, is held in Cambridge annually during the month of October.

chicken cacciatore

DAVE BECKER Chef/Proprietor, Sweet Basil

2   pounds boneless skinless
    chicken thighs

>   Kosher salt and freshly cracked
    pepper to taste

2   tablespoons olive oil

1   Spanish onion, chopped

2   ribs celery, sliced

3   red bell peppers, sliced

2   medium carrots, chopped

10 medium mushrooms, cut into quarters

2   tablespoons minced garlic

4   plum tomatoes, chopped

2   cups chicken stock

1   cup red wine

1   cup port

3/4 cup balsamic vinegar

1   bay leaf

1   to 2 pounds uncooked farfalle or
    other pasta

2   tablespoons unsalted butter

1/3 cup grated asiago or Parmesan cheese
    for garnish

1   bunch fresh basil, chopped for garnish

Season the chicken generously with salt and pepper. Arrange the chicken in a single layer in a roasting pan. Roast at 400 degrees for 20 minutes or until the juices run clear when pricked with a fork.

Heat the olive oil in a saucepan. Add the onion, celery, bell peppers, carrots, mushrooms and garlic. Sauté until the vegetables are browned. Add the tomatoes, stock, wine, port, vinegar and bay leaf. Bring to a boil. Pour over the chicken. Bake for 20 minutes. Remove and discard the bay leaf.

Bring a pot of salted water to a boil. Add the pasta and cook until al dente. Drain, reserving the pasta water; do not rinse the pasta. Add the pasta to the chicken and sauce and stir gently to combine, adding some of the reserved pasta water if the sauce is too dry. If the sauce is too juicy, let it stand until the pasta has absorbed some of the liquid. Add the butter and stir gently until the butter is melted. Adjust the seasonings. Spoon the chicken and sauce into a serving bowl. Garnish with the cheese and basil.

Serves 4 to 6

lemon chicken

2	eggs	2	cups chicken broth
2	cups Italian-style bread crumbs	>	Juice of 6 lemons
8	boneless chicken breasts	1	cup dry white wine
1	tablespoon olive oil	>	Hot cooked rice or egg noodles
1	tablespoon butter		

Beat the eggs lightly in a shallow dish. Place the bread crumbs in a shallow dish. Dip the chicken in the eggs to coat. Dip in the bread crumbs to coat. Heat the olive oil and butter in a large skillet. Cook the chicken in batches in a single layer in the hot oil mixture until brown, turning once. Arrange in a deep 9×13-inch baking dish. Add the broth and lemon juice. Bake, covered, at 350 degrees for 30 minutes. Add the wine. Bake, uncovered, for 30 minutes or until the chicken is cooked through. Serve over rice or noodles.

Serves 6 to 8

chinese-style chicken breasts

1/2	cup chicken broth	1/8	teaspoon pepper
1/4	cup hoisin sauce	1	tablespoon olive oil
2	tablespoons apricot preserves	2	to 3 cups cooked jasmine rice
4	boneless skinless chicken breasts	1/4	cup chopped cashews
1/2	teaspoon salt	1/4	cup chopped green onions

Combine the broth, hoisin sauce and preserves in a bowl; set aside.

Pound the chicken to a thin, uniform thickness; sprinkle with the salt and pepper. Heat the olive oil in a large skillet. Add the chicken. Sauté for 3 minutes on each side; remove from the skillet.

Pour the broth mixture into the skillet. Cook for about 4 minutes or until thickened and heated through, stirring constantly. Return the chicken to the skillet. Cook for 5 to 10 minutes or until the chicken is cooked through. Arrange the rice, chicken and sauce on a serving platter. Sprinkle with the cashews and green onions.

Serves 4

apple-sage chicken

Brimming with the flavors of sweet New England apple cider and fresh sage, this dish is a fall favorite.

1	pound boneless skinless chicken breasts
2	cups apple cider
2	tablespoons butter
4	garlic cloves, minced
2	tablespoons finely chopped fresh sage leaves
1	teaspoon finely chopped fresh rosemary leaves
1	red apple, chopped
>	Salt and pepper to taste
>	Fresh sage leaves for garnish

Combine the chicken and apple cider in a shallow dish. Marinate at room temperature while preparing the remaining ingredients.

Melt the butter in a sauté pan over medium heat. Add the garlic. Cook for 1 minute. Add the undrained chicken, chopped sage and rosemary. Bring to a boil. Reduce the heat to low. Simmer, covered, for about 15 minutes or until the chicken is cooked through, adding the apple during the last few minutes of cooking. Season with salt and pepper. Garnish with sage leaves.

Serves 2 to 4

 Uncommonly Boston — The Schlesinger Library at Harvard University includes a culinary collection of almost 15,000 titles from the United States and around the world.

lobster-stuffed breast of chicken

EXECUTIVE CHEF GERALD BONSEY, CEC   York Harbor Inn, York Harbor, Maine
The succulent lobster stuffing complements the velvety sauce in this spectacular dish.

1/4 cup finely chopped onion	1 teaspoon white pepper
1/4 cup finely chopped celery	8 (6-ounce) boneless skinless chicken breasts, lightly pounded to 1/2-inch thickness
2 tablespoons clarified butter or unsalted butter, melted	
10 ounces butter crackers, crushed	1 pound lobster meat, coarsely chopped
2 tablespoons dry sherry	2 cups heavy cream
1 tablespoon sliced scallions	10 ounces boursin cheese with garlic and herbs, crumbled
1 tablespoon chopped parsley	
1 1/2 teaspoons minced garlic	4 cups cooked jasmine rice
1 1/2 teaspoons Worcestershire sauce	2 pounds asparagus, steamed
1 teaspoon salt	> Sliced scallions

Sauté the onion and celery in the butter in a sauté pan until tender. Add the cracker crumbs, sherry, 1 tablespoon scallions, the parsley, garlic, Worcestershire sauce, salt and white pepper and mix well. Stuff each chicken breast with 1/4 cup of the cracker stuffing and 2 ounces of the lobster, almost wrapping the chicken around the stuffing to create a "ball" and securing with a wooden pick if desired. Place in a baking dish. Bake at 350 degrees for 18 to 20 minutes or until the chicken is cooked through.

Prepare the sauce while the chicken is baking. Bring the cream to a boil in a 2-quart saucepan. Reduce the heat to very low. Whisk in the cheese. Cook very gently until the sauce is slightly thickened, scraping the bottom of the pan frequently with a rubber spatula to prevent burning. The sauce may be held for a short time in a double boiler until ready to serve.

Serve the chicken over the rice and asparagus. Top with the sauce and garnish with scallions.

Serves 8

Uncommonly Boston — The first Thanksgiving was celebrated in Massachusetts in the autumn of 1621 among the Puritans and the native Wampanoag people.

stuffed chicken

6	boneless skinless chicken breasts	2	teaspoons chopped fresh thyme leaves
2	cups finely chopped celery	>	Salt to taste
2	cups finely chopped mushrooms	1	tablespoon olive oil
1 1/2	cups chopped walnuts	>	Freshly squeezed juice of 1 lime
1 1/2	cups bread crumbs	2	cups white wine
1	large onion, finely chopped	1	cup sliced green onions
2	eggs, lightly beaten	1 1/2	cups chicken broth
1	tablespoon chopped garlic	2/3	cup sour cream
2	teaspoons chopped fresh rosemary leaves	2	tablespoons Dijon mustard

Pound the chicken breasts to a uniform thickness; set aside. Combine the celery, mushrooms, walnuts, bread crumbs, onion, eggs, garlic, rosemary, thyme and salt in a bowl. Stuff the chicken breasts with the bread crumb mixture, rolling to enclose the filling; secure with wooden picks.

Brown the chicken in the olive oil in an electric skillet, drizzling each side with lime juice after turning. Add the wine. Bring to a boil. Reduce the heat to low. Simmer, covered, for 10 to 12 minutes or until the chicken is cooked through. Remove the chicken; keep warm in a 150-degree oven. Strain the pan juices; reserve.

Sauté the green onions in the skillet. Add the reserved pan juices and broth. Cook until heated through. Stir in the sour cream and Dijon mustard. Cook until heated through; do not boil. Serve the sauce over the chicken.

Serves 6

Uncommonly Boston — Cambridge resident and culinary pioneer Julia Child aired her first television show, *The French Chef,* on Boston's public television station in 1963.

fricassee de pollo

SOFRITO

2	tablespoons olive oil
1	onion, diced
1/2	green bell pepper, diced
1/2	red bell pepper, diced
4	garlic cloves, minced
1	teaspoon minced fresh oregano leaves
>	Salt and freshly ground pepper to taste

FRICASSEE

1/4	cup flour
1/4	teaspoon salt
1/4	teaspoon paprika
1/8	teaspoon black pepper
1/8	teaspoon cayenne pepper
2 1/2	pounds chicken pieces, skinned
2	tablespoons olive oil
1	cup sofrito
1/2	cup red wine
1/3	cup chopped green olives
1/3	cup chopped kalamata olives
1/4	cup raisins
1/4	cup tomato sauce
2	tablespoons drained capers
>	Salt and freshly ground black pepper to taste
>	Cooked brown or white rice

For the sofrito, heat the olive oil in a skillet over medium heat. Add the onion, bell peppers, garlic and oregano. Sauté for 15 minutes or until the vegetables are very tender. Season to taste with salt and pepper. Set aside 1 cup for the fricassee; discard the remaining sofrito or reserve for another use.

For the fricassee, blend the flour, 1/4 teaspoon salt, the paprika, 1/8 teaspoon black pepper and the cayenne pepper in a sealable plastic bag. Rinse the chicken and pat dry. Add to the plastic bag and shake to coat. Heat the olive oil in a Dutch oven or large deep skillet over medium heat. Add the chicken. Cook until browned on all sides; do not crowd the pan. Remove from the pan; set aside.

Stir in the sofrito, wine, olives, raisins, tomato sauce and capers, scraping up the browned bits from the bottom of the pan. Return the chicken to the pan, stirring to coat with the sofrito mixture. Bring to a boil. Reduce the heat to medium-low. Simmer, covered, for 45 minutes or until the chicken is cooked through. Season with salt and black pepper to taste. Serve over rice.

Serves 6 to 8

To add flavor to chicken parts or a whole roasting chicken before cooking, rub the chicken with a mixture of ground spices and herbs. Another way to impart great flavor is to coat the surface with a compound butter made with softened butter, salt, pepper, and dried herbs.

spicy chicken

in peanut sauce

Marinating chicken is a great way to make it more flavorful and succulent. The acids in marinade cause the poultry tissue to break down, tenderizing the meat and allowing it to retain more moisture.

PEANUT SAUCE

- 1/3 cup peanut butter
- 1/4 cup packed brown sugar
- 1/4 cup soy sauce
- 2 tablespoons vinegar
- 1 tablespoon lime juice
- 2 teaspoons sesame oil

CHICKEN

- 1 tablespoon vegetable oil
- 2 garlic cloves, minced
- 1/2 teaspoon ground ginger
- 1 large onion, sliced
- 1 green bell pepper, cut into 1/4-inch strips
- 2 carrots, thinly sliced
- 2 serrano chiles or Anaheim chiles, diced
- 1 pound boneless skinless chicken breasts, cut into strips
- 2 scallions, diced
- 2 tablespoons fresh cilantro leaves, minced
- 1 teaspoon sesame oil
- 6 cups cooked white rice

For the peanut sauce, combine the peanut butter, brown sugar, soy sauce, vinegar, lime juice and sesame oil in a small bowl. Set aside, covered, for up to 4 hours.

For the chicken, heat the oil in a medium skillet over medium heat. Add the garlic and ginger. Sauté for about 30 seconds or until fragrant. Add the onion, bell pepper, carrots and serrano chiles. Cook for 3 minutes. Add the chicken. Cook for about 5 minutes or until the chicken is cooked through. Whisk the peanut sauce to blend. Stir into the chicken mixture. Cook for 1 minute. Remove from the heat. Stir in the scallions, cilantro and sesame oil. Serve over the rice.

Serves 4

 Uncommonly Boston — The first woman to serve in the U.S. House of Representatives was Edith Nourse Rogers, a Republican from Massachusetts.

chicken spinach casserole

Creamy and delicious, this casserole is appropriate for a simple dinner or a special occasion.

2	pounds fresh spinach, torn into pieces, or 3 (10-ounce) packages frozen chopped spinach, thawed
3	cups chopped cooked chicken breasts
1/4	cup (1/2 stick) butter
3	tablespoons flour
2	cups heavy cream
3/4	cup (3 ounces) shredded Swiss cheese
1	teaspoon grated lemon zest
1	teaspoon lemon juice
1/8	teaspoon mace
>	Dash of Tabasco sauce
1/2	cup bread crumbs
2	tablespoons butter, melted

Cook the spinach; drain. Place in a 7×11-inch baking dish. Top with the chicken. Melt 1/4 cup butter in a saucepan over medium heat. Stir in the flour. Add the cream. Cook until heated through and beginning to thicken, stirring frequently. Remove from the heat. Add the cheese, lemon zest, lemon juice, mace and Tabasco sauce. Stir until the cheese melts and the sauce is well blended. Pour over the chicken and spinach. Combine the bread crumbs and 2 tablespoons butter in a bowl; sprinkle over the top. Bake at 350 degrees for 30 minutes or until heated through. Broil for 5 minutes to brown the top.

Serves 8

Uncommonly Boston — Founded in 1635, Boston Latin School was the first secondary school established in the United States.

curried duck salad

A sweet gewürztraminer pairs beautifully with this spicy and flavorful duck breast.

1   cup mayonnaise

3   tablespoons apricot
    preserves

1   teaspoon curry powder

2   duck breast fillets, cooked,
    cut into 3/4-inch pieces

1   small bunch seedless red
    grapes, cut into halves

1   small bunch seedless green
    grapes, cut into halves

>   Salt and pepper to taste

6   cups mesclun greens

Combine the mayonnaise, preserves and curry powder in a bowl and mix well. Refrigerate, covered, until chilled.

Place the duck and grapes in a bowl. Add the dressing and toss. Season with salt and pepper. Arrange the mesclun on a serving plate and top with the salad.

Note: When cooking boneless duck, allow for 3 to 4 ounces cooked meat per person. Boneless duck yields about three servings per pound after cooking.

Serves 6 to 8

company cornish game hens

The earthy, full-bodied flavors of a rioja are a beautiful complement to game hens or capon.

4   Cornish game hens, split

1   (14-ounce) can beef broth

1/2 cup (1 stick) butter

1/2 cup maple syrup

1/4 cup orange juice

1   tablespoon soy sauce

1   cup grapes

Place the game hens in a roasting pan. Combine the broth, butter, maple syrup, orange juice and soy sauce in a saucepan. Bring to a boil, stirring constantly. Remove from the heat. Pour 1/2 of the sauce over the hens. Roast at 400 degrees for 1 1/4 to 1 1/2 hours or until cooked through, basting with the remaining sauce after 30 minutes and with pan drippings 15 minutes later. Top with the grapes 15 minutes before removing from the oven.

Serves 8

Photo on page 167

Herb-Crusted Rack of Lamb

Meats
& entrées

Kenmore and Brookline have an energy and personality that are uniquely their own. Kenmore and Fenway are often referred to as two different neighborhoods, but they are actually only one. The Kenmore area is home to a burgeoning student population from Berkley College, Simmons College, and Emmanuel College. The neighborhood has a vibrant and eclectic energy that can be attributed to its young residents. Restaurants in the area offer pizza, Chinese take-out, and sushi, and cater to a more hip, late-night crowd. The famous CITGO sign towers above Kenmore Square. Standing sixty feet by sixty feet, the CITGO sign is widely recognized as a symbol of Boston. At one time an energy conservation act forced it to be turned off, but the sign survived in darkness for four years. The sign was rebuilt in 1983 and has been alight ever since. The CITGO sign has stood up to five hurricanes and at one time was made up of more than five miles of neon tubing. Today, thousands of LED lights make the sign more energy efficient. Interestingly, there is no CITGO gas station located beneath this sign.

Fenway Park, the home of the Boston Red Sox, is also located in Kenmore Square. Opened in 1912, Fenway Park is the oldest Major League Baseball field still in use today. Bostonians are Red Sox crazy and have been known to pay premium prices to sit in seats with obstructed views. Daily tours of the park are popular for visitors and locals alike. Baseball purists argue that you haven't experienced the game until you've watched a game at Fenway Park.

Located across the highway is Brookline, a community of 55,000 people within a 6.6-mile radius. It is minutes from the city yet feels less urban than other Boston neighborhoods. Brookline has a large Jewish and Russian population whose cultural and culinary traditions are visible in the many wonderful restaurants and delis located on Beacon Street. The area is home to some of the city's finest kosher butcher shops, whose fresh, pure beef is featured on many holiday tables. Coolidge Corner and Brookline Village are lined with shops and restaurants that are energetic and fun. Coolidge Corner has a 1933 Art Deco theater, which features independent and international films along with documentaries. Brookline is also home to Boston University, the fourth largest private university in America; the birthplace of President John F. Kennedy; and the site of the very first country club in America.

The activities and food of Kenmore and Brookline reflect the tastes and traditions of its energetic, eclectic residents.

herb-crusted rack of lamb

2   large garlic cloves

2   cups dry white bread crumbs

2/3   cup grated pecorino Romano cheese

1/4   cup plus 2 tablespoons Dijon mustard

4   teaspoons fresh rosemary leaves, chopped

1 1/2   teaspoons herbes de Provence

1/4   cup plus 2 tablespoons olive oil

2   (1 1/2-pound) racks of lamb

>   Salt and pepper to taste

Process the garlic in a food processor until minced. Add the bread crumbs, cheese, Dijon mustard, rosemary and herbes de Provence and pulse just until mixed. Remove to a bowl. Drizzle with the olive oil.

Place the lamb bone side up on a baking sheet. Season with salt and pepper. Press the bread crumb mixture onto the lamb.

Roast at 425 degrees for 30 to 40 minutes for medium-rare or until done to taste. Cover with foil. Let rest for 15 minutes before carving.

Serves 4   Photo on page 168

All meats should be allowed to rest, or sit undisturbed, on a cutting board for ten to fifteen minutes after being removed from the oven. Allowing the juices to cool slightly before carving ensures they will not run out of the meat. This helps to keep the meat moist and flavorful.

Uncommonly Boston — The thirty-fifth president, John F. Kennedy, was born in Brookline in 1917 at 83 Beals Street.

springtime roast
leg of lamb

A heavy-gauge pan with two-inch sides should be used when roasting meats. The pan size should suit the roast: If it's too large, the meat can become excessively dry; if too small, the meat can stew in its own juices and become tough.

LAMB

1/3   cup flour

1   teaspoon paprika

>   Salt and freshly ground pepper to taste

1   (4- to 5-pound) boneless leg of lamb, rolled, tied

1   onion, diced

1/2   cup Worcestershire sauce

1/4   cup fresh rosemary leaves

1   tablespoon butter

1   tablespoon lemon juice

2   garlic cloves, minced

GRAVY

3   tablespoons pan drippings

3   tablespoons flour

3   cups beef broth

>   Salt and freshly ground pepper to taste

For the lamb, combine the flour, paprika, salt and pepper. Roll the lamb in the flour mixture. Place in a roasting pan; top with the onion. Roast at 425 degrees for 10 minutes.

Combine the Worcestershire sauce, rosemary, butter, lemon juice and garlic in a saucepan. Bring to a boil. Pour over the lamb. Roast for 10 to 15 minutes longer. Reduce the oven temperature to 325 degrees. Roast until a meat thermometer registers 145 degrees for medium-rare, basting frequently. Let stand, covered with foil, for 10 minutes before carving.

For the gravy, skim the fat from the drippings. Strain the drippings, discarding any solids. Heat in a medium saucepan over medium heat. Whisk in the flour until smooth. Cook for several minutes, stirring constantly. Add the broth gradually. Cook until the gravy reaches the desired consistency, stirring constantly. Season with salt and pepper. Serve with the lamb.

Serves 8

old-fashioned irish stew

1 1/2   to 2 pounds lamb stew meat, cut into bite-size pieces

2   teaspoons olive oil

4   cups water

2   cups sliced peeled potatoes

2   cups sliced carrots

2   cups diced turnips

1   large yellow onion, sliced

1/2   to 1 teaspoon marjoram

1/2   to 1 teaspoon thyme

1/2   to 1 teaspoon rosemary, crushed

1/8   teaspoon pepper

Brown the lamb in the olive oil in a Dutch oven over medium-high heat. Add the water. Bring to a boil. Reduce the heat to low. Simmer, covered, for 1 hour.

Add the potatoes, carrots, turnips, onion, marjoram, thyme, rosemary and pepper. Bring to a boil. Reduce the heat to low. Simmer, covered, for 30 to 40 minutes or until the vegetables are tender. Adjust the seasonings to taste.

Serves 6

 Uncommonly Boston — Fenway Park is home to one of the last hand-operated scoreboards in Major League Baseball.

cassoulet

MARK ORFALY   Chef and Co-owner, Pigalle Restaurant

Chef Orfaly prepares classic French cuisine served simply and with elegance. In true Parisian style, he combines the finest, freshest ingredients with traditional cooking techniques to produce dishes that are flavorful, complex, and luxurious.

DUCK CONFIT

> Curing salt

4   duck legs

> Duck fat or olive oil

CASSOULET

1   pound dried white beans

2   lamb shanks

> Olive oil

3   large white onions, chopped

5   ribs celery, chopped

3   carrots, chopped

2   leeks, white and green parts only, chopped

6   garlic cloves, chopped

1   bunch fresh thyme

1   bunch fresh tarragon

1   (750-milliliter) bottle dry white wine

6   cups (about) veal stock

4   pork sausage links

> Bread crumbs for topping

> Fresh herbs for garnish

For the duck confit, sprinkle curing salt on both sides of the duck legs. Place on a baking sheet; cover with plastic wrap. Refrigerate for 8 to 12 hours. Pat the duck dry with a clean kitchen towel. Place the duck in a baking dish. Add enough duck fat to completely cover the duck legs. Bake at 250 degrees for 8 hours or until the duck is tender to the bone and the skin is slightly browned; set aside.

For the cassoulet, sort and rinse the beans. Place in a bowl and add enough cold water to cover. Soak for 8 to 12 hours; drain and set aside.

Sear the lamb shanks in a generous amount of olive oil in a large sauté pan over high heat until browned. Remove from the pan; set aside. Add the onions, celery, carrots, leeks and garlic to the pan. Cook until tender. Spoon the cooked vegetables in the center of a piece of cheesecloth; top with the thyme and tarragon. Tie the cheesecloth into a bundle with butcher's twine; set aside.

Drain any drippings from the sauté pan. Add the wine and stir to deglaze the pan, gently scraping up the browned bits from the bottom. Cook until the wine is reduced by ¹/₂. Add the lamb shanks, beans and vegetable bundle, immersing the bundle down into the center. Add enough stock to cover generously. Bring to a simmer. Bake, covered, at 350 degrees for 3 hours or until the shanks are tender to the bone. When cool enough to handle, remove and discard the vegetable bundle. Remove the meat from the bones and reserve the beans in the cooking liquid.

Poach the sausage links in simmering water in a saucepan for 4 to 5 minutes or until firm to the touch.

To assemble the cassoulet, layer the ingredients as follows in four individual baking dishes. Spoon the beans with cooking liquid generously over the bottom of each dish to cover. Add a large piece of lamb, 1 sausage link and 1 duck leg. Bake at 350 degrees for 15 minutes or until hot and bubbly. Top with bread crumbs. Bake for 5 minutes or until browned. Garnish with herbs and serve immediately.

Notes: Duck fat is usually available from your local butcher. The cassoulet may also be assembled and baked in one large baking dish.

Serves 4

Uncommonly Boston — In the early 1900s, Brookline was known as the town of millionaires.

grilled marinated lamb chops

A full-bodied shiraz or merlot balances the richness of lamb and other heavy meats.

1/3	cup finely chopped fresh thyme leaves
1/3	cup finely chopped fresh oregano leaves
1/4	cup finely chopped fresh rosemary leaves
6	large garlic cloves, crushed
2	tablespoons coarse salt
1 1/2	cups olive oil
1	cup fresh lemon juice
>	Freshly ground pepper to taste
8	lamb chops

Combine the thyme, oregano, rosemary, garlic and salt using a mortar and pestle or in a food processor until a coarse paste forms. Whisk in the olive oil and lemon juice. Season with pepper.

Arrange the lamb chops in a single layer in a shallow baking dish. Pour the garlic mixture over the chops. Marinate, covered, in the refrigerator for 4 to 6 hours, turning once. Remove the lamb chops from the marinade, reserving the marinade. Let stand until near room temperature. Grill over hot coals for a few minutes per side or to the desired degree of doneness, turning once and brushing with the marinade before turning; discard any remaining marinade.

Serves 4

Uncommonly Boston — The official nickname of Massachusetts is the Bay State or Old Bay State.

christmas beef tenderloin
with bordelaise sauce

BORDELAISE SAUCE

1/4	cup (1/2 stick) butter
2	large onions, thinly sliced
2	carrots, thinly sliced
2	garlic cloves, minced
2	sprigs of flat-leaf parsley
15	peppercorns
4	whole cloves
1	large bay leaf
1/4	cup flour
2 3/4	cups beef broth
1/2	cup red wine
2	teaspoons chopped fresh flat-leaf parsley
1	teaspoon kosher salt
1/4	teaspoon freshly ground pepper

TENDERLOIN

1	(5- to 6-pound) beef tenderloin roast, trimmed, at room temperature
1/4	cup (1/2 stick) butter, softened
4	ounces freshly ground Dunkin' Donuts Coffee
1	to 2 tablespoons kosher salt
1	to 2 tablespoons freshly ground pepper
1	tablespoon paprika

For the bordelaise sauce, melt the butter in a large saucepan over medium-high heat. Add the onions, carrots, garlic, parsley sprigs, peppercorns, cloves and bay leaf. Sauté for 8 to 10 minutes or until the onions are tender and golden brown. Reduce the heat to low. Stir in the flour. Cook until the flour is lightly browned, stirring constantly. Stir in the broth. Bring to a boil. Reduce the heat to low. Simmer until the sauce is smooth and thickened, stirring frequently. Pour through a strainer into a bowl, pressing on the solids to force as much of them into the sauce as possible; discard the remaining solids. Stir in the wine, chopped parsley, salt and ground pepper. Refrigerate, covered, for 8 to 12 hours. Reheat in a saucepan over low heat prior to serving.

For the tenderloin, tie the thin tail end of the beef under to make the roast a uniform thickness. Place in a roasting pan. Spread the butter over the entire surface of the beef. Combine the coffee, salt, pepper and paprika in a bowl. Sprinkle over the beef to coat. Roast at 500 degrees for about 5 minutes per pound or until a meat thermometer registers 120 degrees for rare or until done to taste. Cover loosely with foil and let stand for about 30 minutes. Carve into slices and serve with the bordelaise sauce.

Serves 8 to 10

roasted beef tenderloin
with merlot jus

ANTHONY E. DAWODU Executive Chef, 33 Restaurant & Lounge

Chef Dawodu is known for peppering traditional New England cuisine with hints of the exotic. He uses the best locally grown produce and freshly caught seafood. His results are perfect homemade pasta and flavorful sauces that provide his customers with magical dining experiences.

MERLOT JUS

5	shallots, diced
1	tablespoon vegetable oil
4	cups veal stock
2	cups merlot
3	sprigs of fresh thyme
1	tablespoon cornstarch
1	tablespoon water

HORSERADISH REMOULATA

1	tablespoon freshly grated horseradish
1	teaspoon chopped fresh thyme leaves
1	teaspoon grated lemon zest
1	teaspoon sea salt

BEEF

4	(8-ounce) beef tenderloin fillets
>	Salt and pepper to taste
1	tablespoon vegetable oil
1	tablespoon butter

VEGETABLES

1	pound wild mushrooms, coarsely chopped or sliced
1	pound peeled fingerling potatoes, cooked, sliced
12	peeled asparagus spears, cooked, cut into 1-inch pieces
1	tablespoon vegetable oil

For the merlot jus, sauté the shallots in the oil in a saucepan until browned. Add the stock, wine and thyme sprigs. Bring to a boil. Reduce the heat to low. Simmer for 1 hour. Strain the sauce; return to the saucepan. Combine cornstarch and water in a small bowl and mix well. Stir 1 tablespoon into the sauce. Cook until thickened; keep warm.

For the horseradish remoulata, combine the horseradish, thyme, lemon zest and sea salt in a bowl; set aside.

For the beef, season the fillets with salt and pepper. Sear the fillets on both sides in the oil and butter in a large sauté pan. Roast at 425 degrees for 10 minutes or until done to taste.

For the vegetables, sauté the mushrooms, potatoes and asparagus in the oil in a large sauté pan. Place on a plate and arrange the fillets on top. Drizzle the merlot jus around the plate along with a touch of horseradish remoulata.

Serves 4

herb-roasted beef tenderloin

1 tablespoon freshly ground pepper

1 (2 1/2- to 3-pound) beef tenderloin roast, trimmed, at room temperature

1/4 cup fresh flat-leaf parsley leaves, minced

1 1/2 tablespoons minced fresh chives

1 1/2 teaspoons dried thyme

> Salt to taste

Rub the pepper over the entire surface of the beef. Combine the parsley, chives and thyme and press onto the beef to coat. Season with salt. Tie the thin tail end of the beef under to make the roast a uniform thickness. Place in a roasting pan. Roast at 425 degrees for about 30 minutes or until a meat thermometer registers 155 degrees for medium or until done to taste. Let stand for 15 to 20 minutes. Carve into thin slices.

Serves 6 to 8

red chile-marinated skirt steak

TONY MAWS   Executive Chef and Owner, Craigie Street Bistrot

Chef Maws strives to combine the philosophy and style of the Parisian Bistrot Moderne culinary movement with local and organic ingredients from New England. His talent and unique approach offer diners exceptional and creative food that is near perfection.

6 dried New Mexico red chiles

1 tablespoon coriander seeds

1 tablespoon cumin seeds

1 tablespoon dried thyme

1 tablespoon ground ginger

2 teaspoons peppercorns

10 allspice berries

2 whole cloves

6 garlic cloves

1 cup canola oil

1/2 cup soy sauce

> Salt to taste

5 pounds skirt steaks

Rehydrate the chiles in boiling water; drain and remove the seeds. Grind the coriander seeds, cumin seeds, thyme, ginger, peppercorns, allspice and cloves. Combine the ground seasonings, chiles, garlic, canola oil, soy sauce and salt in a food processor or blender and process until puréed. Rub the chile mixture over the skirt steak. Place in a shallow baking dish. Marinate, covered, in the refrigerator for 8 to 12 hours. Remove the steak from the marinade, discarding the marinade. Grill the steak to the desired degree of doneness.

Serves 10

beef braciole in tomato sauce

1 1/2 pounds flank steak, skirt steak or top round steak

2 garlic cloves, finely chopped

3/4 cup (3 ounces) grated Parmesan cheese

1/2 cup fresh parsley leaves, chopped

1/2 teaspoon salt

1/2 teaspoon freshly ground black pepper

1/4 to 1/3 cup olive oil

2 1/2 cups canned peeled crushed tomatoes

1/4 teaspoon (about) basil

1/4 teaspoon (about) red pepper flakes

1/4 teaspoon (about) mint

> Salt and freshly ground black pepper to taste

2 tablespoons chopped fresh parsley for garnish

Pound the steak lightly with a meat mallet into 1/2-inch thickness, keeping the meat in one piece. Top with the garlic. Combine the cheese, 1/2 cup parsley, 1/2 teaspoon salt and 1/2 teaspoon black pepper in a bowl. Sprinkle over the garlic. Roll up the steak starting at the short side in jelly roll fashion; tie securely with butcher's twine or secure with several wooden picks.

Heat the olive oil in a large, heavy pot over medium heat. Add the beef braciole. Cook for about 10 minutes or until browned on all sides. Add the tomatoes, basil, red pepper and mint. Season with salt and black pepper to taste. Bring to a boil. Reduce the heat to low. Simmer, covered, for about 1 hour or until the beef is tender. Do not overcook or it will fall apart. Remove the braciole to a cutting board. Let stand for about 5 minutes.

Remove the string or wooden picks from the braciole. Carve crosswise into 1/3-inch-thick slices. Arrange on a platter. Ladle the sauce over the top. Garnish with 2 tablespoons parsley.

Serves 6

Photo on page 181

Uncommonly Boston — There is a seat in the right field bleachers at Fenway Park that is painted red. This marks the spot where the ball landed from the longest measurable home run that was ever hit inside Fenway Park.

beef stir-fry with coconut rice

Creamy coconut milk is a great counterpoint to the spicy sauce in this easy stir-fry.

RICE

- 1 (14-ounce) can light coconut milk
- 1 cup water
- 1 teaspoon minced garlic
- 1/4 teaspoon salt
- 1/8 teaspoon cayenne pepper
- 1 cup jasmine or other short grain white rice

STIR-FRY

- 2 tablespoons white wine
- 2 tablespoons low-sodium soy sauce
- 1 tablespoon cornstarch
- 1 tablespoon water

- 1 tablespoon chili-garlic sauce
- 1 tablespoon balsamic vinegar
- 1 pound flank steak, trimmed
- 1 tablespoon dark sesame oil
- 1 large onion, sliced vertically (about 1 1/2 cups)
- 3 cups broccoli florets
- 1 bunch asparagus, diagonally sliced
- 1 large red bell pepper, sliced (about 1 cup)
- 3 green onions, thinly sliced
- 1/4 teaspoon pepper
- 1/4 cup fresh cilantro leaves, chopped

For the rice, combine the coconut milk, water, garlic, salt and cayenne pepper in a saucepan. Bring to a boil. Stir in the rice. Simmer, covered, for 18 minutes or until the liquid is absorbed.

For the stir-fry, combine the wine, soy sauce, cornstarch, water, chili-garlic sauce and vinegar in a bowl; set aside.

Cut the steak across the grain into 1/4-inch strips. If the strips are too long, cut them into halves. Heat 1 teaspoon of the sesame oil in a wok or large skillet over high heat. Add 1/2 of the beef. Stir-fry until almost cooked through. Remove from the wok; keep warm. Repeat with the remaining beef and 1 teaspoon of the sesame oil.

Heat the remaining 1 teaspoon sesame oil in the wok. Add the onion. Stir-fry for about 8 minutes or just until tender. Add to the beef; keep warm. Heat the wok. Add the broccoli, asparagus, bell pepper and green onions. Stir-fry for 5 minutes or until tender-crisp. Season with the pepper. Return the beef and onion to the wok. Add the soy sauce mixture. Cook until the mixture is heated through and the sauce thickens, stirring constantly. Remove from the heat; stir in the cilantro. Serve over the rice.

Serves 4 to 6

grilled marinated steak tips

Great on the barbecue, these steak tips are ideal on a summer day.

2	pounds sirloin steak tips	2	tablespoons orange juice or pineapple juice
1/3	cup soy sauce		
1/4	cup sesame oil	1	to 2 tablespoons minced garlic
2	tablespoons brown sugar	1	teaspoon red pepper flakes
2	tablespoons sesame seeds	>	Grated zest of 1 orange
2	tablespoons chopped gingerroot	1/2	teaspoon dry mustard
2	tablespoons vegetable oil	1/4	teaspoon cayenne pepper

Place the steak tips in a sealable plastic bag. Whisk the soy sauce, sesame oil, brown sugar, sesame seeds, gingerroot, vegetable oil, orange juice, garlic, red pepper, orange zest, dry mustard and cayenne pepper in a bowl. Pour over the steak; seal the bag. Marinate in the refrigerator for 1 hour, turning the bag over once.

Remove the steak from the marinade and pat dry; discard the marinade. Grill over medium-hot coals for 5 to 6 minutes; turn. Grill for 5 to 6 minutes longer. Move the steak to a cooler area of the grill. Grill until done to taste. Cover loosely with foil. Let stand for 5 minutes before carving.

Serves 6

Uncommonly Boston — The first municipal fire alarm system using a telegraph was installed in Boston in 1852.

nor'easter beef stew

Hearty and economical, this beef stew is great for serving the whole family.

When making soups and stews with meat, economical cuts may be used since the long simmering time allows the meat to tenderize and to give its full flavor to the dish.

2	pounds beef stew meat
>	Salt and pepper to taste
1	tablespoon olive oil
3	large onions, coarsely chopped
2	bay leaves
1	teaspoon thyme
2	ounces tomato paste
2	cups baby carrots, cut into halves
2	teaspoons minced garlic
6	red potatoes, peeled, cut into quarters
2	(15-ounce) cans low-sodium beef broth or consommé
1	cup water
2	tablespoons Chinese black vinegar or Worcestershire sauce
>	Parsley for garnish

Season the beef with salt and pepper. Heat the olive oil in a 6-quart pot over medium heat. Add the beef. Sauté for 10 minutes or until browned on all sides. Remove from the pot with a slotted spoon. Add the onions, bay leaves and thyme to the beef drippings. Sauté for about 10 minutes or until the onions are tender. Add the tomato paste, carrots and garlic. Sauté over medium-high heat for 3 minutes. Stir in the beef, potatoes, broth, water and vinegar. Bring to a boil. Reduce the heat to low. Simmer, covered, for 1 1/2 hours or until the beef is fork-tender, stirring occasionally. Remove and discard the bay leaves. Garnish with parsley.

Serves 4 to 6

braised beef short ribs
with vanilla-glazed carrots

ANA SORTUN   Chef/Owner, Oleana Restaurant

Chef Sortun's menu has received local and national praise and features unique Arabic-influenced foods of the Mediterranean. She uses the highest quality spices in unusual combinations to layer her dishes with subtle and exotic flavors.

8	beef short ribs		1/2	cup packed brown sugar
1/4	cup kosher salt		2	tablespoons tamarind paste
1	large onion, coarsely chopped		1	cup hot water
1	carrot, coarsely chopped		2	tablespoons butter
1	bay leaf		1/2	vanilla bean
1	cup medium-bodied non-oaky white wine (such as a dry riesling)		4	carrots, diagonally sliced 1/2 inch thick
1	cup balsamic vinegar		1/2	cup water
1	tablespoon chopped garlic (about 3 cloves)		>	Salt and pepper to taste
			1	tablespoon fresh lemon juice

Season the short ribs generously with 1/4 cup salt. Place in a single layer in a large, heavy roasting pan. Top with the onion, chopped carrot and bay leaf. Combine the wine, vinegar, garlic and brown sugar in a small bowl; pour over the short ribs. Place the tamarind paste in the same bowl. Whisk in 1 cup hot water to slightly dissolve and loosen the tamarind. Add to the short ribs. The liquid in the roasting pan should come 3/4 of the way up the sides of the short ribs. Add more water to the pan if necessary. Cover the pan tightly with a double layer of foil. Braise at 350 degrees for 3 hours or until the short ribs are fork-tender and falling apart. Remove the short ribs to a serving dish.

Strain the braising liquid through a sieve into a tall pitcher. Refrigerate for at least 1 hour so the fat solidifies on the surface. Remove and discard the fat. Pour the cooking liquid into a large, deep sauté pan. Bring to a boil over high heat. Add the short ribs. Reduce the heat to medium-low. Simmer for 15 minutes or until the sauce thickens and glazes the short ribs; keep warm.

Melt the butter in a medium sauté pan over medium heat. Scrape the seeds from the vanilla bean into the butter. Add the carrots and 1/2 cup water. Season with salt and pepper to taste. Cook over low to medium heat for about 10 minutes or until the carrots are tender and glazed. Stir in the lemon juice. Adjust the seasonings. Turn the short ribs over in the sauce with tongs to make them glazed and sticky. Place each on a plate and top with a little of the sauce. Serve with the glazed carrots.

Serves 8

palmer ridge ranch meat loaf

GLAZE

- 1/4 cup packed brown sugar
- 1/4 cup cider vinegar
- 1/4 cup ketchup
- 1/4 cup chili sauce

MEAT LOAF

- 2 teaspoons vegetable oil
- 1 yellow onion, chopped
- 1/2 cup chopped green bell pepper
- 2 garlic cloves, minced
- 1/2 cup (or more) plain yogurt
- 2 eggs
- 2 teaspoons Dijon mustard
- 2 teaspoons Worcestershire sauce
- 1 teaspoon salt
- 1/2 teaspoon thyme
- 1/2 teaspoon freshly ground pepper
- 1/4 teaspoon Tabasco sauce
- 1 pound ground chuck
- 1/2 pound ground pork
- 1/2 pound ground veal
- 1 1/3 cups fresh bread crumbs
- 1/3 to 1/2 cup chopped fresh herbs (parsley, thyme, oregano)
- 6 to 8 slices bacon

For the glaze, combine the brown sugar, vinegar, ketchup and chili sauce in a saucepan. Bring to a simmer; set aside.

For the meat loaf, heat the oil in a skillet. Add the onion, bell pepper and garlic. Sauté until tender; set aside.

Combine the yogurt, eggs, Dijon mustard, Worcestershire sauce, salt, thyme, pepper and Tabasco sauce in a large bowl. Add all the ground meat and mix well. Add the bread crumbs, herbs and onion mixture. Stir with a fork. If the mixture sticks to the bowl, add more yogurt. With wet hands, pat the meat mixture into a 5×9-inch loaf pan. Brush with 1/2 of the glaze. Cut the slices of bacon to the width of the pan. Arrange the bacon crosswise over the top.

Bake at 350 degrees for about 1 hour or until the bacon is crisp and the meat loaf is cooked through. Cool for 15 to 20 minutes before cutting. Reheat the remaining glaze and serve with the meat loaf.

Serves 6 to 8

veal-stuffed eggplant

> Salt to taste

2 (1-pound) globe eggplant, cut lengthwise into halves

1/4 cup extra-virgin olive oil

1 cup ground veal or ground turkey (about 8 ounces)

2 to 3 garlic cloves, cut into halves

4 ripe tomatoes, thinly sliced

2 cups chicken broth

1 cup arborio rice

1 teaspoon marjoram

1 teaspoon thyme

> Pepper to taste

1/4 cup (1 ounce) grated pecorino cheese

2 tablespoons chopped fresh parsley for garnish

> Grated pecorino cheese for garnish

Sprinkle salt over the cut sides of the eggplant. Let drain, salted sides down, in a colander for 30 minutes.

Heat 2 tablespoons of the olive oil in a large saucepan over medium heat. Add the ground veal. Sauté for 3 to 4 minutes. Add the garlic. Sauté until tender. Stir in two of the sliced tomatoes and 1/2 cup of the broth. Bring to a boil. Reduce the heat to low. Simmer, covered, for 5 minutes.

Rinse the eggplant. Scoop out most of the flesh, reserving the eggplant shells. Chop the flesh; add to the veal mixture and mix well. Stir in the rice, marjoram, thyme and 1 cup of the broth and mix well. Simmer, covered, over medium-low heat for 15 minutes, stirring frequently. Remove and discard the garlic halves; season with salt and pepper to taste.

Pour the remaining 2 tablespoons olive oil over the bottom of a large baking sheet. Place the eggplant shells on the baking sheet. Arrange the remaining two sliced tomatoes around the eggplant. Spoon the rice mixture into the shells. Pour the remaining 1/2 cup broth around the eggplant.

Bake at 350 degrees for about 40 minutes or until the eggplant are tender, basting them with pan juices occasionally. Sprinkle with 1/4 cup cheese. Bake for 5 to 10 minutes longer. Serve garnished with the parsley and additional cheese.

Serves 4

Uncommonly Boston — Boston is a city of colleges, with over one hundred colleges and universities located in the greater metropolitan area.

baked ham with glazed apricots

The apricots in this dish impart a complex flavor.

1	pound dried apricots
1	cup madeira
1	(12- to 16-pound) bone-in ready-to-eat ham
>	Whole cloves
1/4	cup Dijon mustard
1	cup packed dark brown sugar
3	cups apple juice
>	Mustards
>	Chutneys

Combine the apricots and madeira in a small saucepan. Bring to a boil. Remove from the heat and cover. Let stand.

Peel the skin from the ham and trim the fat, leaving about a 1/4-inch layer. Score the fat in a diamond pattern, using diagonal lines about 1 inch apart. Set the ham in a shallow baking pan. Insert a clove in the crossed point of each diamond. Pat the Dijon mustard evenly over the top and sides of the ham. Sprinkle with brown sugar. Pour the apple juice into the pan. Bake at 350 degrees for 1 hour, basting every 10 to 15 minutes. Add the undrained apricots. Bake for 30 minutes, basting every 10 to 15 minutes.

Place the ham on a large platter. Attach the apricots to the top of the ham with wooden picks in a decorative fashion if desired. Skim the fat from the pan juices and pour the pan juices into a sauceboat. Serve with mustards, chutneys and pan juices.

Serves 20 to 25

out-of-the-park pork tenderloin

3/4 cup fresh lemon juice

1/2 cup soy sauce

6 tablespoons honey

2 shallots, cut into halves

2 garlic cloves, cut into halves

2 bay leaves, crumbled

2 teaspoons freshly ground pepper

1 teaspoon dry mustard

1 teaspoon chopped fresh parsley

1/2 teaspoon salt

1/2 teaspoon ground ginger

3 pounds pork tenderloin

Combine the lemon juice, soy sauce, honey, shallots, garlic, bay leaves, pepper, dry mustard, parsley, salt and ginger in a food processor and process until puréed. Place the pork in a shallow dish. Pour the marinade over the pork, turning to coat. Marinate, covered, in the refrigerator for 8 to 12 hours, turning occasionally.

Drain the pork, reserving the marinade. Grill the pork for about 20 minutes or until a meat thermometer registers 160 degrees, turning frequently. Remove to a serving platter; cover with foil. Pour the reserved marinade into a saucepan. Bring to a boil. Boil for about 5 minutes or until slightly reduced. Slice the pork and serve with the heated marinade.

Serves 8

bourbon pork tenderloin

1/4 cup packed brown sugar

1/4 cup Jack Daniel's Whiskey

1/4 cup soy sauce

1/4 cup peanut oil

1/4 cup Dijon mustard

3 garlic cloves, minced

1 teaspoon minced gingerroot

1 teaspoon Worcestershire sauce

2 (1-pound) pork tenderloins

Combine the brown sugar, whiskey, soy sauce, peanut oil, Dijon mustard, garlic, gingerroot and Worcestershire sauce in a large sealable plastic bag. Reserve and refrigerate 1/4 cup of the marinade for basting. Add the pork; seal the bag. Marinate in the refrigerator for 8 to 12 hours, turning the bag over once or twice. Let the pork stand at room temperature for 30 minutes before grilling. Remove the pork from the marinade; discard the marinade. Grill or broil 6 inches from the heat source for 15 to 25 minutes or until a meat thermometer registers 160 degrees, turning often and basting frequently with the 1/4 cup reserved marinade. Carve into 1/2-inch slices.

Serves 6

pork tenderloin
with remoulade sauce

The crisp, fresh qualities of a Samuel Adams Boston Lager provide a nice balance to the richness of this pork recipe.

To ensure that pork is well cooked, follow the cooking time and temperature instructions on the recipe. Use a meat thermometer to measure the internal temperature of the meat and check for doneness. The recommended internal temperature for pork is 160 degrees.

BRINE

6	cups water
1/4	cup sugar
1/4	cup salt
>	Handful of peppercorns
2	tablespoons gin, or handful of juniper berries
>	Herbs to taste
2	pork tenderloins

REMOULADE SAUCE

1/2	cup mayonnaise
1/4	cup sour cream
3	tablespoons Dijon mustard
1	tablespoon chopped sweet pickles or gherkins
1	tablespoon drained chopped capers
1	tablespoon chopped fresh parsley
1	teaspoon tarragon
>	Olive oil
>	Freshly ground pepper to taste

For the brine, combine the water, sugar, salt, peppercorns, gin and herbs in a bowl, stirring until the sugar and salt are dissolved. Add the pork. Refrigerate, covered, for 8 to 12 hours. Do not leave the pork in the brine for more than 48 hours or the meat will become too salty.

For the remoulade sauce, combine the mayonnaise, sour cream, Dijon mustard, pickles, capers, parsley and tarragon in a bowl. Refrigerate, covered, until ready to serve.

Remove the pork from the brine about 30 minutes before grilling; blot dry. Rub with olive oil and pepper. Preheat a gas grill to high. Place the pork on the grill. Reduce the temperature to medium-low. Grill for 20 to 30 minutes or until a meat thermometer registers 160 degrees, turning once or twice. Cover with foil. Let stand for 15 minutes. Carve into slices and serve with remoulade sauce.

Serves 6 to 8

maple mustard barbecue
pork chops

1/2	cup dark amber maple syrup	8	(1-inch) center-cut boneless pork loin chops
1/4	cup spicy brown mustard	>	Extra-virgin olive oil
1/4	cup apple cider	>	Salt and pepper to taste
1/4	onion, finely chopped	3	Golden Delicious apples, sliced crosswise 1/2-inch thick (do not peel or core)
1	teaspoon cumin		
1/2	teaspoon ground allspice	>	Grill seasoning blend

Combine the maple syrup, mustard, apple cider, onion, cumin and allspice in a small saucepan. Cook over medium heat for 5 minutes or until the sauce begins to thicken.

Coat the pork chops lightly with olive oil. Season with salt and pepper. Heat a grill pan or nonstick griddle over medium-high heat. Add the pork. Cook for 3 minutes per side. Baste liberally with the sauce. Cook for 2 to 3 minutes more. Remove the pork to a baking sheet; baste again with the sauce. Bake at 350 degrees for 10 to 12 minutes or until the pork is cooked through.

Coat the sliced apples with a drizzle of olive oil. Season with grill seasoning or salt and pepper. Cook, in batches, on the grill pan for 3 minutes on each side or just until tender. To serve, arrange the pork chops and apples on a platter.

Serves 8

The freshest pork chops have a fine grain and reddish-pink color. The external fat should be creamy and white and have no dark spots or blemishes. Never buy pork chops that are soft, pale, pinkish-gray, or overly wet.

Pumpkin Cheesecake

DESSERTS
& cookies

The neighborhoods of Roxbury, Jamaica Plain, and Dorchester have a shared history, unique in Boston's urban landscape.

Roxbury was originally connected to Boston by a narrow strip of land, the "Roxbury Neck." Founded in 1630, Roxbury became a city in 1848 and was annexed to the city of Boston in 1868. The area prospered because land traffic had to pass through Roxbury to reach Boston. Throughout the eighteenth century, Roxbury was known as a farming community famous locally for its fruit trees. The Williams apple and the Roxbury russet were local favorites. In the nineteenth century, Roxbury became an industrial area and growing suburb. Factories developed in the northern part of Roxbury, and a diverse immigrant population arrived. With the introduction of electric trolley service in 1887, Roxbury became the first suburb accessible by streetcar in the U.S. In the twentieth century, Roxbury became the center of Boston's African-American community. Today, this urban neighborhood reflects the cultural influences of its residents. Small neighborhood restaurants feature Creole, Haitian, and Southern soul food.

Although they are recognized today as separate neighborhoods, Jamaica Plain was once part of Roxbury. Jamaica Plain, commonly referred to as "JP," has an identity and history all its own. At the center of this community is Jamaica Pond, whose pure waters provided a cool refuge to nineteenth-century Bostonians. In the 1850s, mansions were built as summer cottages for the rich; single-family homes were built for the middle classes; and triple-decker houses were constructed for immigrant workers. Today, Jamaica Plain is urban and eclectic. The businesses along its main thoroughfare have both a metropolitan and an ethnic flair. Restaurants feature a mix of Irish-American, Latin, Mexican, and Caribbean cuisine. A great way to sample the flavors of Jamaica Plain is to visit a neighborhood cafe, bakery, or restaurant for delicious desserts with an exotic flair.

Settled in 1630, Dorchester was independent of the city of Boston until 1870. It began as a farming community that cultivated the Dorchester blackberry, Dower cherry, and President Wilder strawberry. Small commercial and industrial businesses developed along the Neponset River. Dorchester has been known for its industry, but it is best remembered for its world-famous chocolate. In 1765, the Walter Baker Chocolate Company was founded in an old sawmill on the banks of the Neponset River. By 1842, the Lower Mills section of Dorchester was known as "Chocolate Village," because it was home to three chocolate factories. Baker Chocolate was manufactured in Dorchester for two centuries until the company was sold in 1965. Today, its distinctive flavor and vivid orange box are reminders of the proud legacy of Dorchester and Baker Chocolate.

Visit Roxbury, Jamaica Plain, and Dorchester to experience their unique urban flair and imaginative, delicious desserts.

pumpkin cheesecake

CRUST

1/2	cup graham cracker crumbs
1/2	cup finely chopped pecans
1/3	cup gingersnap crumbs
1/4	cup granulated sugar
1/4	cup packed light brown sugar
5	tablespoons butter, melted, cooled

FILLING

1 1/2	cups canned pumpkin
3	eggs
1/2	cup packed light brown sugar
1 1/2	teaspoons cinnamon
1/2	teaspoon salt
1/2	teaspoon ginger
1/2	teaspoon nutmeg
1/2	teaspoon cloves
24	ounces cream cheese, softened, cut into small cubes
1/2	cup granulated sugar
2	tablespoons heavy cream
1	tablespoon cornstarch
1	tablespoon vanilla extract
1	tablespoon bourbon

TOPPING

2	cups sour cream
3	tablespoons sugar
1	tablespoon bourbon
16	pecan halves for garnish

To cut neat cheesecake slices, use a sharp, thin-bladed knife dipped into hot water. Shake off any excess drops of water before slicing. Remember to clean the knife and dip it into hot water after each slice.

For the crust, combine the graham cracker crumbs, pecans, gingersnap crumbs, granulated sugar and brown sugar in a bowl. Stir in the butter. Press onto the bottom of a 9-inch springform pan. Chill in the freezer for 20 minutes.

For the filling, whisk the pumpkin, eggs, brown sugar, cinnamon, salt, ginger, nutmeg and cloves in a bowl; set aside. Cream the cream cheese and granulated sugar in a large bowl. Beat in the cream, cornstarch, vanilla and bourbon. Add the pumpkin mixture and beat until smooth. Pour into the chilled crust.

Bake at 350 degrees for 50 to 55 minutes or until the center is set. Cool in the pan on a wire rack for 5 minutes.

For the topping, whisk the sour cream, sugar and bourbon in a bowl. Spread over the top of the cheesecake. Bake for 5 minutes longer. Cool completely. Refrigerate, covered, for 8 to 12 hours. To serve, remove the side of the pan. Garnish with the pecans.

Serves 12

Photo on page 192

black walnut apple cake

2	cups granulated sugar		1	teaspoon baking soda
3/4	cup vegetable oil		1/2	teaspoon salt
1/4	cup milk		3	cups finely chopped peeled apples
3	eggs		1	cup chopped black walnuts or English walnuts
2	teaspoons vanilla extract			
3	cups flour		1/2	cup confectioners' sugar (optional)
2	teaspoons cinnamon			

Combine the granulated sugar, oil, milk, eggs and vanilla in a large bowl with a wooden spoon. Sift the flour, cinnamon, baking soda and salt together. Add to the egg mixture and stir until blended. Stir in the apples and walnuts. Pour into a greased and floured bundt pan. Bake at 325 degrees for 1 hour and 20 minutes to 1 1/2 hours or until the cake tests done. Cool in the pan for 15 minutes. Invert onto a wire rack to cool completely. Sift the confectioners' sugar over the top before serving.

Serves 10

blueberry cake

1 1/2	cups sugar		3	cups flour
3/4	cup vegetable oil		1	tablespoon baking powder
3	eggs		1	(21-ounce) can blueberry pie filling
>	Juice of 1 orange (about 1/2 cup)		3	tablespoons sugar
1	teaspoon vanilla extract		1	teaspoon cinnamon

Combine 1 1/2 cups sugar, the oil, eggs, orange juice and vanilla in a bowl. Combine the flour and baking powder; add to the egg mixture and mix well. Spread about 1/3 of the batter in a greased 9×13-inch cake pan. Top with the pie filling, spreading to completely cover the batter. Carefully spread the remaining batter over the pie filling. If the batter becomes too thick to spread, stir in a small amount of orange juice. Mix 3 tablespoons sugar and the cinnamon in a small bowl. Sprinkle the cinnamon-sugar over the top of the cake. Bake at 350 degrees for 10 minutes. Reduce the oven temperature to 325 degrees. Bake for 40 minutes or until a wooden pick inserted into the center comes out clean. Let stand until cool. This is best if it stands overnight.

Serves 12

orange almond cake
with chocolate ganache frosting

A Junior League of Boston favorite!

TOPPING

1/3 cup blanched sliced almonds

2 teaspoons unsalted butter, softened

2 tablespoons sugar

CAKE

1 cup sugar

3 eggs

> Grated zest of 1 large orange

1/8 teaspoon salt

1/8 teaspoon almond extract

1 1/4 cups flour

1 1/2 teaspoons baking powder

1/3 cup heavy cream

3 tablespoons unsalted butter, melted, cooled

5 tablespoons amaretto

GANACHE

1 cup (6 ounces) semisweet chocolate chips

6 tablespoons brewed coffee

> Pinch of salt

6 tablespoons unsalted butter, cut into small pieces

For the topping, place the almonds on a baking sheet. Bake at 325 degrees for 5 to 10 minutes or until lightly browned; cool. Grease a 2×8-inch round cake pan with the butter. Press the almonds into the butter on the bottom of the pan. Sprinkle with the sugar and set aside. Increase the oven temperature to 375 degrees.

For the cake, beat the sugar, eggs, orange zest, salt and almond extract in a large bowl at high speed for about 4 minutes or until thick and pale yellow. Sift the flour and baking powder over the top and fold into the egg mixture. Stir in the cream and butter. Pour into the prepared pan. Bake at 375 degrees for 30 to 35 minutes or until a wooden pick inserted into the center comes out clean. Cool in the pan on a wire rack for 10 minutes. Loosen the cake from the side of the pan. Invert onto a plate. Pierce the surface of the cake all over with a wooden skewer. Spoon the amaretto over the top. Cool completely.

For the ganache, melt the chocolate with the coffee and salt in the top of a double boiler or in a microwave until smooth. Remove from the heat. Add the butter two to three pieces at a time, stirring until the mixture is completely smooth. Let stand at room temperature until cooled to 90 degrees. Spread over the cooled cake.

Serves 10

chocolate-walnut whiskey cake

CAKE

1   (2-layer) package chocolate cake mix

1   (4-ounce) package chocolate or
     fudge instant pudding mix

1/2   cup vegetable oil

1/2   cup brewed coffee

1/2   cup whiskey, bourbon or rum

3   eggs

1/2   cup chocolate chips

1/2   cup chopped walnuts

GLAZE

1/2   cup (1 stick) butter

1   cup sugar

1/4   cup brewed coffee

1/2   cup whiskey, bourbon or rum

For the cake, combine the cake mix, pudding mix, oil, coffee, whiskey and eggs in a large bowl and mix well. Fold in the chocolate chips and walnuts. Pour into a greased bundt pan. Bake at 350 degrees for about 40 minutes or until the cake tests done. Cool in the pan on a wire rack.

For the glaze, combine the butter, sugar and coffee in a small saucepan. Heat until the butter melts and the sugar dissolves completely. Remove from the heat. Stir in the whiskey. Pour the hot glaze over and around the cake in the pan. When the glaze is absorbed, remove the cake from the pan.

Serves 16

cream cheese pound cake

1 1/2   cups (3 sticks) butter, softened

8   ounces cream cheese, softened

3   cups sugar

3   cups minus 2 tablespoons flour

6   eggs

1   tablespoon vanilla extract

1/8   teaspoon salt

Cream the butter and cream cheese in a bowl. Add the sugar 1 cup at a time, beating until smooth. Add the flour 1 cup at a time alternately with 2 eggs at a time, beating until smooth. Beat in the vanilla and salt. Pour into a greased and floured bundt pan. Bake at 325 degrees for 1 1/4 hours or until a wooden pick inserted into the center of the cake comes out clean. Do not overbake. Cool in the pan for 10 minutes. Invert onto a wire rack to cool completely.

Serves 12

milk chocolate fondue

SCOTT GAMBONE   Executive Chef, JER-NE, The Ritz-Carlton, Boston Common

Chef Gambone reintroduces classic American favorites with his signature style. His contemporary flair and many delightful culinary surprises make dining at JER-NE a "journey" worth taking.

18	ounces high-quality milk chocolate	1/2	cup heavy cream, cold
1	cup sugar	1 1/2	ounces Grand Marnier
1/2	cup water	>	Marshmallows, pound cake pieces and strawberries for dipping
1/4	cup light corn syrup		

Chop the chocolate into 1/2-inch pieces. Place in a stainless steel or heatproof glass bowl; set aside.

Combine the sugar, water and corn syrup in a saucepan. Bring to a boil. Cook until the sugar is completely dissolved. Pour over the chocolate and whisk until completely melted and smooth with a consistent color. Stir in the cream and then the Grand Marnier. (May be prepared up to 1 week in advance. Refrigerate, covered, until ready to use. Gently reheat in the microwave or in the top of a double boiler.)

Pour the chocolate mixture into a fondue pot heated with a tea light. Do not use a stronger flame or the chocolate may scorch. Serve with marshmallows, pound cake and strawberries for dipping.

Serves 4

Uncommonly Boston — The Fig Newton was first produced in and named after the town of Newton, Massachusetts, in 1891. Neither the taste, shape, nor size of Fig Newtons has been changed in more than one hundred years.

cardamom crème brûlée

2	cups heavy cream	1	teaspoon freshly ground cardamom
8	egg yolks	1	teaspoon vanilla extract
1/2	cup granulated sugar	1/4	cup packed brown sugar

Fill a 9×13-inch baking pan halfway with water. Place in the oven on the center rack. Preheat the oven to 300 degrees.

Heat the cream in a medium saucepan over medium heat until almost boiling, stirring occasionally. Whisk the egg yolks into the cream one at a time. Add the granulated sugar and whisk briefly. Remove from the heat. Stir in the cardamom and vanilla. Cool slightly. Pour through a fine sieve to strain out any cardamom pieces. Pour into six custard cups or ramekins. Carefully place the custard cups in the hot water in the baking pan. The water should come halfway up the sides of the cups. Bake at 300 degrees for 50 minutes. Cool slightly. Refrigerate, covered, for at least 6 hours or up to 2 days. Just before serving, sprinkle with the brown sugar. Broil on the upper oven rack for 2 minutes or until the sugar is crunchy. Refrigerate for 5 minutes and serve.

Serves 6

Photo on page 200

baked apple crisp

The crisp, sweet flavor and full body of a sauterne or riesling would pair beautifully with this baked fruit dessert.

1	cup sugar	1/2	cup (1 stick) butter
3/4	cup flour	4	cups sliced Granny Smith apples
1/2	teaspoon cinnamon	1/4	cup orange juice
1/4	teaspoon nutmeg	>	Vanilla ice cream
>	Dash of salt		

Combine the sugar, flour, cinnamon, nutmeg and salt in a bowl. Cut in the butter until crumbly; set aside.

Place the apples in a 9-inch pie plate. Pour the orange juice over the apples. Top with the crumb mixture. Bake at 375 degrees for about 45 minutes or until golden brown. Cool for 5 to 10 minutes. Serve with ice cream.

Serves 4 to 6

hanover street tiramisu

Some chefs like to assemble and measure out each ingredient ahead of time before cooking. Organize ingredients in small containers for quick use.

5	egg yolks	1	tablespoon fresh lemon juice
3	tablespoons granulated sugar	1	teaspoon vanilla extract
1	tablespoon dark rum, or to taste	5	tablespoons double-strength brewed Dunkin' Donuts Coffee
1	cup mascarpone cheese, softened		
3	egg whites	5	tablespoons confectioners' sugar
2	tablespoons granulated sugar	16	ladyfingers
1/3	cup whipping cream	>	Baking cocoa for dusting

Beat the egg yolks with 3 tablespoons granulated sugar in a bowl until thick and pale yellow. Add the rum and beat until well blended. Blend in the cheese until smooth and light; do not overbeat. Set aside.

Beat the egg whites with 2 tablespoons granulated sugar in a bowl until stiff, glossy peaks form. Fold into the cheese mixture. Beat the cream in a bowl until stiff peaks form. Fold into the cheese mixture gently with the lemon juice and vanilla; set aside.

Whisk the coffee and confectioners' sugar in a shallow bowl until the sugar is completely dissolved. Dip both sides of eight ladyfingers briefly into the coffee mixture. Arrange in a single layer in an 8×8-inch baking dish. Top with 1/2 of the cheese mixture. Repeat with the remaining eight ladyfingers and cheese mixture. Dust the top with baking cocoa. Refrigerate, covered, for 4 to 12 hours before serving.

Note: To avoid uncooked eggs that may carry salmonella, we suggest using an equivalent amount of pasteurized egg substitute.

Serves 10 to 12

Uncommonly Boston — The NECCO candy company, located in Revere, Massachusetts, manufactures eight billion Sweethearts® conversation hearts each year, which are sold primarily between January 1 and Valentine's Day.

kahlúa-chocolate
cream torte

1	package angel food cake mix	3	tablespoons butter
2	pints whipping cream	2	ounces unsweetened chocolate
1	teaspoon cornstarch	1	cup (6 ounces) chocolate chips
3/4	cup Kahlúa or coffee-flavored liqueur	3/4	cup sugar
1/4	cup sugar	3	tablespoons milk
3	ounces cream cheese	1	teaspoon vanilla extract

When melting chocolate, make sure that no moisture or water comes into contact with it. Just a few drops of water can make the chocolate seize and become difficult to use.

Prepare the cake mix using the package directions. Pour into two 9-inch round cake pans. Bake and cool as directed on the package. Split each cake layer horizontally into halves; set aside.

Beat the cream with the cornstarch in a bowl until stiff peaks form. Reserve 1/4 of the whipped cream in a small bowl. Beat the remaining whipped cream for 1 minute longer, adding the Kahlúa and 1/4 cup sugar gradually.

Spread the Kahlúa whipped cream between the layers and over the top and side of the cake. Refrigerate the frosted cake.

Melt the cream cheese, butter, unsweetened chocolate and chocolate chips in the top of a double boiler. Remove from the heat. Stir in 3/4 cup sugar, the milk and vanilla. Cool slightly. Fold into the reserved whipped cream. Freeze for 10 minutes or until firmed up slightly. Pour decoratively over the frosted cake. Refrigerate the cake until ready to serve.

Serves 12

Uncommonly Boston — The first supermarket in America was founded in Dorchester, Massachusetts.

berry pudding
with rum whipped cream

PUDDING

1	pint fresh strawberries, sliced
1 1/2	cups sugar
1/4	cup water
3	cups fresh raspberries
2	cups fresh blueberries
2	tablespoons framboise (raspberry brandy) or Chambord
1	(1- to 1 1/2-pound) loaf brioche, challah or Portuguese sweet bread, cut into 1/2-inch slices, crusts removed

RUM WHIPPED CREAM

1	cup heavy whipping cream, cold
3	tablespoons sugar
1	tablespoon dark rum
1/2	teaspoon vanilla extract

For the pudding, combine the strawberries, sugar and water in a large saucepan. Cook over medium-low heat for 5 minutes. Add 2 cups of the raspberries and the blueberries. Bring to a simmer, stirring occasionally. Simmer for 1 minute. Remove from the heat. Stir in the remaining 1 cup raspberries and framboise. Let stand for 15 minutes or until cooled. Spoon 1/2 cup of the berry mixture onto the bottom of a 3×7 1/2-inch round soufflé dish. Arrange some of the bread slices in an attractive pattern over the berry mixture, cutting the slices to fit if necessary (this will be the top of the pudding after unmolding). Continue layering the berry mixture and bread until all the ingredients are used; the top layer should be berries. Cover loosely with plastic wrap. Weight the pudding by placing a plate the same diameter as the inside of the dish on top; place a heavy can on the plate. Refrigerate for 7 to 8 hours. Remove the plate and can. Cover tightly with plastic wrap. Refrigerate for 8 to 12 hours longer.

For the rum whipped cream, beat the cream in a mixing bowl until it starts to thicken. Add the sugar, rum and vanilla and beat until stiff peaks form.

To serve, loosen the pudding from the side of the dish. Invert onto a serving plate. Cut into wedges and serve with the whipped cream or ice cream.

Serves 8

Photo on page 205

Uncommonly Boston — The official state cookie is the Toll House cookie.

cranberry trifle

2	cups ground cranberries		1	cup sugar
2	large bananas, chopped		1/2	cup (1 stick) butter, softened
1/2	cup sugar		2	eggs
2	cups crushed vanilla wafers		1/2	cup chopped pecans
6	tablespoons butter or margarine, melted		1	cup heavy whipping cream

Combine the cranberries, bananas and 1/2 cup sugar in a bowl; set aside. Combine the vanilla wafer crumbs and melted butter in a bowl. Reserve 3 tablespoons. Press the remaining crumb mixture onto the bottom of a glass trifle dish; set aside. Cream 1 cup sugar and 1/2 cup butter in a bowl until light and fluffy. Beat in the eggs. Fold in the pecans. Spread over the crumb crust. Top evenly with the cranberry mixture. Beat the cream in a bowl until soft peaks form. Spread over the cranberry mixture. Sprinkle with the reserved crumb mixture. Refrigerate, covered, for 1 to 3 hours.

Note: To avoid uncooked eggs that may carry salmonella, we suggest using an equivalent amount of pasteurized egg substitute.

Serves 6 to 8

raspberry-eggnog trifle

2	(4-ounce) packages vanilla instant pudding mix		1 1/2	teaspoons vanilla extract
3 1/2	cups eggnog		1	purchased angel food cake, cut into cubes
1/4	teaspoon nutmeg		2	(12- to 16-ounce) packages frozen raspberries
2	cups heavy whipping cream			
2	tablespoons confectioners' sugar		24	whole graham crackers, crushed

Chill a mixing bowl and beaters in the freezer for 5 to 10 minutes. Prepare the pudding mixes using the package directions, substituting the eggnog for the milk. Blend in the nutmeg; set aside. Beat the cream with the confectioners' sugar in the chilled bowl until soft peaks form. Fold in the vanilla. Layer 1/3 of the angel food cake, 1/3 of the pudding, 1 1/2 cups of the raspberries, 1/4 of the graham cracker crumbs and 1/3 of the whipped cream in a trifle dish or straight-sided glass bowl. Repeat the layers twice to form three layers. Garnish with the remaining raspberries and graham cracker crumbs. Chill before serving.

Serves 24

cranberry mousse

8 cups cranberries

2 1/2 cups granulated sugar

1 1/2 cups water

1/4 cup fresh orange juice

1 tablespoon fresh lemon juice

5 (1/4-ounce) envelopes unflavored gelatin

4 cups heavy whipping cream

1/4 cup confectioners' sugar

1 1/2 teaspoons vanilla extract

Combine the cranberries, granulated sugar and water in a saucepan. Bring to a boil. Cook for 4 to 5 minutes or until the cranberries pop.

Combine the orange juice and lemon juice in a bowl. Soften the gelatin in the juices. Add the gelatin mixture to the hot cranberries and stir until dissolved. Chill until cold and partially set.

Beat the cream in a bowl until soft peaks form, adding the confectioners' sugar and vanilla gradually. Fold into the cranberry mixture. Pour into a freezer-proof serving bowl. Freeze until firm.

Serves 25

Good, ripe cranberries are shiny and plump and range in color from light to dark red. Shriveled berries or those with brown spots should be discarded. Fresh cranberries may last up to two months in the refrigerator. Cooked cranberries can be kept in a covered container in the refrigerator for up to a month. Washed cranberries may be frozen and kept in an airtight bag in the freezer for up to one year.

Uncommonly Boston — The official state dessert is Boston Cream Pie.

chocolate mousse cake

The rich, silky textures and flavors of Samuel Adams Cream Stout or Samuel Adams Chocolate Bock provide a subtle complement to this luxurious dessert.

Chocolate can be melted in the microwave oven. Heat dark chocolate at 50 percent power and milk and white chocolate at 30 percent power. Stir the chocolate every fifteen seconds, heating just until it is melted.

CRUST

- 2   cups chocolate sandwich cookie crumbs
- 1/2 cup sugar
- 1/2 cup (1 stick) butter, melted

FILLING

- 2   cups (12 ounces) chocolate chips
- 1/2 cup (1 stick) butter
- 3   egg yolks, lightly beaten
- 3   tablespoons Kahlúa (optional)
- 1   pint heavy whipping cream
- 3   egg whites
- >   Pinch of cream of tartar

For the crust, combine the cookie crumbs, sugar and butter in a bowl. Reserve 1/4 cup for the topping. Press the remaining crumb mixture onto the bottom and side of a 9-inch springform pan. Bake at 350 degrees for 8 minutes; cool.

For the filling, place the chocolate chips and butter in a large microwave-safe bowl. Microwave on Medium at 2-minute intervals or just until melted, stirring between each interval; cool. Stir in the egg yolks and Kahlúa.

Beat the cream in a small bowl until stiff peaks form. Refrigerate until chilled. Wash the beaters thoroughly. Beat the egg whites with the cream of tartar in another small bowl until stiff peaks form. Fold into the chocolate mixture gently. Do not overmix; there should be some visible streaks of egg white. Fold in the chilled whipped cream gently but thoroughly. Do not overmix. Pour into the crust. Sprinkle with the reserved crumb mixture. Refrigerate, covered, for at least 6 hours.

To serve, loosen the crust from the side of the pan with a warm knife; remove the side from the pan. Remove the cake to a serving plate.

Note: To avoid uncooked eggs that may carry salmonella, we suggest using an equivalent amount of pasteurized egg substitute.

Serves 8

cranberry-pecan praline
tart with chocolate-coconut crust

RUTH-ANNE ADAMS Executive Chef, Casablanca Restaurant

Chef Adams is known for the outstanding quality and presentation of her award-winning Mediterranean fare. Her meat and fish dishes are infused with north African and southern European flavors and served in a casually sophisticated, romantic environment.

PASTRY SHELL

- 3/4 cup plus 1 tablespoon butter, softened
- 4 ounces sugar (about 1/2 cup)
- 1 egg
- 1 egg yolk
- 1/2 teaspoon vanilla extract
- 12 ounces pastry flour (about 1 1/2 cups)
- 1/3 cup baking cocoa, sifted
- > Pinch of salt
- 2 tablespoons shredded coconut, toasted

FILLING AND TOPPING

- 1/2 cup sugar
- 1/2 cup corn syrup
- 1/4 cup (1/2 stick) butter, melted
- 2 eggs, lightly beaten
- 1 1/2 teaspoons flour
- 1/2 teaspoon vanilla extract
- > Pinch of salt
- 1 1/2 cups pecans, toasted, coarsely chopped
- 1/2 cup shredded coconut, toasted
- 2 cups cranberries
- 1/4 cup sugar
- > Sweetened crème fraîche (optional)

For the pastry shell, cream the butter and sugar in a bowl. Add the egg, egg yolk and vanilla, mixing well after each addition. Add the pastry flour, baking cocoa and salt and mix just until blended. Stir in the coconut. Shape the dough into a large disk. Refrigerate, wrapped in plastic wrap, for 1 hour or until chilled. Spray a 9 1/2-inch tart pan with a removable bottom with nonstick cooking spray. Roll the dough on a lightly floured surface 11 1/2 inches in diameter and 1/4 inch thick. Fit into the prepared pan. Refrigerate for 30 minutes. Place pie weights in the pastry shell. Bake at 350 degrees for 7 minutes.

For the filling, whisk 1/2 cup sugar, the corn syrup, butter, eggs, flour, vanilla and salt in a bowl. Stir in the pecans and coconut. Pour into the prebaked pastry shell.

For the topping, sauté the cranberries with 1/4 cup sugar in a skillet over medium heat just until the sugar is melted. The cranberries should remain whole. Spoon evenly over the top of the tart. Bake at 350 degrees for 15 minutes or until the edge is set and the center resembles gelatin. Let stand until cooled. Serve with crème fraîche.

Serves 8

pecan tartlets

1/2	cup (1 stick) butter, softened	1	teaspoon vanilla extract
3	ounces cream cheese, softened	2/3	cup dark corn syrup
1	cup flour	2	eggs
1/2	cup packed brown sugar	1	cup chopped pecans
1/4	cup (1/2 stick) butter, softened		

Combine 1/2 cup butter, the cream cheese and flour in a bowl. Chill, wrapped in plastic wrap, for 30 minutes. Divide the dough into thirty-two equal portions. Shape each portion into a ball. Press over the bottoms and sides of miniature muffin cups. Cream the brown sugar, 1/4 cup butter and the vanilla in a bowl. Beat in the corn syrup and eggs. Stir in the pecans. Spoon into the prepared crusts (there may be some filling left over). Bake at 375 degrees for 18 minutes or until the filling is bubbly and dark brown and the crust is golden brown. Cool in the pan on a wire rack. Loosen the tartlets from the side of the cups with a knife and remove.

Serves 8

lumberjack cookies

These cookies are chewy, spicy, and delicious!

1	cup (2 sticks) butter, softened, or 1 cup shortening	2	teaspoons cinnamon
1	cup sugar	1	teaspoon baking soda
2	eggs	1	teaspoon salt
1	cup dark molasses	1	teaspoon ginger
4	cups sifted flour	1/2	cup sugar

Cream the butter and 1 cup sugar in a bowl until light and fluffy. Beat in the eggs. Add the molasses and mix well. Sift the flour, cinnamon, baking soda, salt and ginger together. Add the dry ingredients to the creamed mixture gradually and mix well. Do not overmix.

Shape by teaspoonfuls into balls. Roll in 1/2 cup sugar. Place on a lightly greased cookie sheet. Bake at 350 degrees for 12 to 15 minutes or until lightly browned around the edges. Cool on a wire rack.

Serves 36 to 48

double chocolate cookies

NICOLE COADY Executive Pastry Chef, Finale

Chef Coady creates delectable works of art at the country's only upscale desserterie. She feels that familiar flavors and taste are the most important elements to a good dessert. The desserts she creates are both beautiful and delicious.

8 1/2	ounces semisweet chocolate	1 1/2	teaspoons vanilla extract
3	ounces bittersweet chocolate	1/2	cup flour
1/2	cup (1 stick) unsalted butter	1/4	teaspoon baking powder
1 1/4	cups sugar	1/4	teaspoon salt
3	eggs		

Melt the semisweet chocolate, bittersweet chocolate and butter in the top of a double boiler, stirring occasionally until blended; set aside.

Beat the sugar, eggs and vanilla in a bowl until thick and pale yellow. Sift the flour, baking powder and salt together. Add the chocolate mixture gradually to the egg mixture, beating at low speed. Fold in the flour mixture gradually. The cookie batter will be liquid. Refrigerate, covered, for 3 hours.

Lightly spray a cookie sheet with nonstick cooking spray. Drop the batter by rounded tablespoonfuls at least 3 inches apart onto the prepared cookie sheet. Place another ungreased cookie sheet underneath for insulation. Bake at 350 degrees for 10 to 15 minutes or until the center is firm to the touch (cake-like firmness). Do not overbake; the cookies should be moist and chewy. For best results, bake as close to serving time as possible.

Serves 24

Uncommonly Boston — In 1801, the first copper works in America was founded by Paul Revere in Dorchester, Massachusetts.

melting pot cookies

1 cup (2 sticks) unsalted butter, softened
3/4 cup granulated sugar
3/4 cup packed light brown sugar
1 tablespoon vanilla extract
1 tablespoon coffee-flavored liqueur
1 tablespoon Frangelico
2 eggs
2 1/2 cups flour
1 teaspoon baking soda
1/2 teaspoon salt
2 cups (12 ounces) milk chocolate chips
1 cup (6 ounces) semisweet chocolate chips
1 cup English toffee bits or butterscotch chips
1 cup chopped walnuts
1/2 cup chopped pecans
1/2 cup chopped hazelnuts

Cream the butter, granulated sugar, brown sugar, vanilla, coffee-flavored liqueur and Frangelico in a bowl at medium speed until light and fluffy. Beat in the eggs. Combine the flour, baking soda and salt. Add to the creamed mixture and stir to make a soft dough. Stir in the milk chocolate chips, semisweet chocolate chips, toffee bits, walnuts, pecans and hazelnuts. Drop by 1/4 cupfuls 2 inches apart onto a lightly greased cookie sheet. Bake at 325 degrees for 16 to 18 minutes. Cool on the cookie sheet briefly. Remove to a wire rack to cool completely.

Note: May omit Frangelico and increase coffee-flavored liqueur to 2 tablespoons.

Serves 24

Uncommonly Boston — In 1639, the first free American public school, The Mather School, was founded in Dorchester, Massachusetts.

orange-chocolate macaroons

An updated version of a classic cookie.

1	cup flour
1	teaspoon baking powder
1/4	teaspoon salt
2/3	cup sugar
3	ounces cream cheese, softened
1/4	cup (1/2 stick) butter, softened
1	egg
1	teaspoon vanilla extract
3/4	teaspoon almond extract
1/2	teaspoon grated orange zest, or 1/4 teaspoon orange oil
3 3/4	cups (about 12 ounces) shredded coconut
2	cups (12 ounces) chocolate chips

Combine the flour, baking powder and salt; set aside. Cream the sugar, cream cheese and butter with a mixer until light and fluffy. Beat in the egg, vanilla, almond extract and orange zest. Add the flour mixture and stir just until blended. Stir in 2 1/2 cups of the coconut and 1 cup of the chocolate chips.

Place the remaining 1 1/4 cups coconut in a bowl. Drop walnut-sized pieces of the dough into the coconut and roll to coat. Place on a cookie sheet lined with baking parchment or waxed paper. Bake at 275 degrees for 40 to 50 minutes or until lightly browned. Cool on a wire rack for 15 minutes. Remove to a wire rack to cool completely.

Melt the remaining 1 cup chocolate chips in the top of a double boiler. Drizzle over the macaroons with the tines of a fork. Let stand until the chocolate is set.

Serves 36

Contributors

The Junior League of Boston gratefully acknowledges the
generous recipe contributions of our friends, families, and members.

Kirsten Alexander	Catherine Bruce Konuah	Sarah Cunningham	Sue Gallagher
Christine Anastos	Cara Mia Bruncati	Tricia Curtin	Denise Gavern
Kennon Anderson	Jennifer Buck	Michelle Davis	Shawna Giggey-Mashal
Tara Auclair	Dana Burgess	Diana Delaney	Susie Gillis
Cheryl Balian	Megan Burling	Lynda Dennen	Roberta Gilmour
Katherine Ball Bassick	Leah Busque	Karen DiMarzo	Mary Grace
Sarah Ruth Barnard	Elizabeth Butcher	Karen Diombala	Kristin Greene
Tyler Battaglia	Sara Cadena	Rebecca Dominguez	Jessica Grosman
Suzanne Battit	Sneha Campanella	Sally Donovan	Leanne Hannon
Julie-Ann Baumer	Mary Canby	Daphne Durham	Judy Harrington
Greer Bautz	Noel Cappillo	Cherie Bosarge Dutton	Jennifer Harris
Kristi Baxter	Sigrid Carroll	Catharine Ebling	Amanda Hartmann
Dave Becker	Pamela Choi	Barbara Larmon Failing	Christine Hayes
Tamara Belmonte	Erin Clement	Sarah Feather	Kerry Healey
Anne Benning	Florence Clement	Rachel Finke	Haidee Heyward
Lorrie Berry	Kevin Clement	Hilary Forbes	Renee Hoffmeister
Carole Berutti	Alice Clements	Lisa Formicola	Corina Hopkins
Pamela Berutti	Amy Cohen	Paula Fowler	Katherine Howe
Linda Bloh	Susan Copelas	Melissa Fox	Lyn Huckabee
Gerald Bonsey	Katie Corrigan	Stan Frankenthaler	Melisa Hudson
Lesa Botti	Heather Crofts	Margo Friedman	Liz Humphreys McCarthy
Dedee Bowers	Helene Crofts	Anna Furman	Hollie Hurwitch
Fawn Boyd Vigil	Alison Cromer	Shannon Furrow	Diane Hutchins-Fridmann

Heather Jackson	Kirby Lunger	Molly Ousey	Amelia Slawsby
Abigail Johnson	Lisa Macchi	Jennifer Packard	Else Slepecky
Adrienne Johnston	Catherine Madden	April Paterno	Ashley Smith
Abigail Joslin	Emily Malone	Muffy Pease	Coleen Smith
Cindy Joyce	Peggy Mangan-Cross	Michele Pelino	Ada Stauffer
Lucy Kapples	Lisa Martin	Karen Pevenstein	Melissa Stevens
Mary Kayser	Margaret May	Nancy Phinney	Lisa Christine Summerville
Hilary Keates	Carla Blakely McDonough	Karen Postal	Alicia Talanian
Jennifer Keller	Paul McDonough	Tatum Pyle	Lisa Tasker
Ashley King	Kimberly McKillop	Jennifer Reber	Cesarina Templeton
Mary Kittell	Matt McKillop	Markus Ripperger	Allison Thies
Nissa Knight	Julian Median	Christy Roach	Marissa Thomis
Eileen Krebs	Katherine Menzia	Claire Rosebush	Vyctoria Thwreatt
Rachel Krebs	Lisa Merriman	Frauke Roth	Jane Timothy
Jeanne Kuespert	Erinn Michalek	Virginia Russell	Molly Toland
Jennifer Landry	Kelley Mongeau	Margaret Rutter	Elizabeth Traverso
Julie LeBlanc	Peter Mongeau	Emily Sah	Ming Tsai
Diane L'Ecuyer	Kathleen Mrachek Leland	Jennifer Samson	Elizabeth Tyminski
Kelly L'Ecuyer	Diane Murphy	Shannon Sardelli	Teresa Voght
Christopher Leu	Stephanie Murphy	Lynne Schaffer	Katy Weber
Meredith Levin	Stephanie Murray	Leanne Scott	Jan Paula Wehlage
Jennifer Lewis	Marybeth Nelson	Nancy Seibel	Lisa Wesley
Rebecca Lindland	Melissa Nott	Heather Shaff Beaver	Robin Westropp
Beth Llewellyn	Janna O'Neill	Julie Shea	Jennifer Wheaton
Karen Roth LoRusso	Jamie O'Riordan	Ashley Shepardson	Christie Whitcomb
Sandra Ludeke	Jennifer Orr	Annie Sigal	Nora Wilkes

Resources

33 Restaurant & Lounge
33 Stanhope Street, Boston, MA 02116
Phone 617-572-3311
33Restaurant.com

75 Chestnut
75 Chestnut Street, Boston, MA 02108
Phone 617-227-3675
75chestnut.com

Aujourd'hui
Four Seasons Hotel
200 Boylston Street, Boston, MA 02116
Phone 617-338-4400
fourseasons.com/boston/vacations/dining_56.html

blu at the sports club
4 Avery Street, Boston, MA 02111
Phone 617-375-8550
blurestaurant.com

Blue Ginger
583 Washington Street, Wellesley, MA 02482
Phone 781-283-5790
Ming.com/blueginger

Casablanca
40 Brattle Street, Cambridge, MA 02138
Phone 617-661-1373
Casablanca-Restaurant.com

Catch
34 Church Street, Winchester, MA 01890
Phone 781-729-1040
CatchRestaurant.com

Chez Henri
One Shepard Street, Cambridge, MA 02138
Phone 617-654-8980
chezhenri.com

Craigie Street Bistrot
5 Craigie Circle, Cambridge, MA 02459
Phone 617-964-2819
craigiestreetbistrot.com

Finale Desserterie & Bakery
One Columbus Avenue, Boston, MA 02116
Phone 617-423-3184
finaledesserts.com

Hampshire House
84 Beacon Street, Boston, MA 02108
Phone 617-227-9600
hampshirehouse.com

Legal Sea Foods
255 State Street, Boston, MA 02109
Phone 617-227-3115
Legalseafoods.com
(Additional locations throughout Boston)

Oleana
134 Hampshire Street, Cambridge, MA 02139
Phone 617-661-3336
OleanaRestaurant.com

Parker's Restaurant
The Omni Parker House Hotel
60 School Street, Boston, MA 02108
Phone 617-227-8600
ParkerHouseBoston.com

Pigalle
75 Charles Street South, Boston, MA 02116
Phone 617-423-4944
pigalleBoston.com

Sweet Basil
942 Great Plain Avenue, Needham, MA 02492
Phone 781-444-9600

The Ritz-Carlton
Boston Common, On Avery at Tremont
10 Avery Street, Boston, MA 02111
Phone 617-574-7100
Ritzcarlton.com

The Union Oyster House
41 Union Street, Boston, MA 02108
Phone 617-227-2750
UnionOysterHouse.com

Turner Fisheries
Westin Copley Place
10 Huntington Avenue, Boston, MA 02116
Phone 617-424-7425

Upstairs on the Square
91 Winthrop Street, Cambridge, MA 02138
Phone 617-864-1933
UpstairsOnTheSquare.com

Dunkin' Brands
130 Royall Street, Canton, MA 02021
781-737-3000
dunkindonuts.com
(Parent company of Dunkin' Donuts)

The Boston Beer Company
75 Arlington Street, 5th Floor, Boston, MA 02116
617-368-5080
bostonbeer.com

On Holiday, LLC
Dresswear for the
Socially Responsible Woman
77 Barley Neck Road, Orleans, MA 02653
508-255-0605
onholidaydresswear.com

Menus

St. Patrick's Day Parade

Sunday's Best Bloody Mary

Goat Cheese Torta*

Baked Cherry Tomatoes*

Pork Tenderloin with Bourbon Sauce

Boston Baked Beans

Irish Soda Bread

Black Walnut Apple Cake

Boston Marathon Party

Rasmopolitan

Prosciutto and Swiss Hors d'Oeuvre

Artichoke Dip

Arugula Salad

Pasta Primavera with Shrimp*

Hanover Street Tiramisu

Summer Roof/Deck Party!

Chilled white wine

Artichoke Crostini with Brie

Tomato Salad

Cumin and Cilantro Corn Skillet*

Pecan-Crusted Salmon*

Berry Pudding with Rum Whipped Cream*

Espanade Fourth of July Picnic

Summer Splendor

Deviled Eggs with Prosciutto and Capers*

Tuscan Bean Insalata

Greek Pasta Salad

Chicken Salad on the Charles

Crusty French bread

Melting Pot Cookies

Head of the Charles Regatta Party

Fall Rum Punch

Three Pepper Quesadillas

Pumpkin Cider Soup

Turkey Burgers with Apple and Brie*

Chocolate Mousse Cake

Boston Beanpot Hockey Tournament

Robust red wine

Tapenade on Crostini

Field Greens with Cranberries and Walnuts

Herb-Crusted Rack of Lamb*

Refrigerator Mashed Potatoes*

Steamed haricots verts

Pumpkin Cheesecake

Winter Skating Party

Creamy Hot Chocolate*

Red-Nosed Reindeer

Vidalia Onion Dip

Hearty Fish Chowder*

Crusty French bread

Mixed field greens with vinaigrette

Almond Biscotti

Baked Apple Crisp

* Photo recipe

Index

* Indicates a photo recipe

BOSTON
uncommon

a culinary journey

through Boston's

distinctive

neighborhoods

The Junior League of Boston
117 Newbury Street
Boston, Massachusetts 02116
617-536-9640

BOSTON uncommon _____ at $29.95 per book $ _____

Postage and handling at $4.50 per book $ _____

Total $ _____

Please make check payable to The Junior League of Boston.

_____
Name

_____
Street Address

_____
City   State   Zip

_____
Telephone

_____
E-mail

Books may also be ordered using a credit card at
the Junior League of Boston Web site, www.JLBoston.org.

Photocopies will be accepted.